The Village of Cannibals

The Village of Cannibals

Rage and Murder in France, 1870

Alain Corbin

Translated by Arthur Goldhammer

Harvard University Press
Cambridge, Massachusetts
1992

Copyright © 1992 by the President and Fellows of Harvard College
All rights reserved
Printed in the United States of America
10 9 8 7 6 5 4 3 2 1

This book was originally published as *Le Village des cannibales,* by
Aubier-Montaigne, copyright © 1990 by Aubier-Montaigne.

This book is printed on acid-free paper, and its binding materials
have been chosen for strength and durability.

Library of Congress Cataloging-in-Publication Data

Corbin, Alain.
[Village des cannibales. English]
The village of cannibals: rage and murder in France, 1870 /
Alain Corbin; translated by Arthur Goldhammer.
p. cm.
Translation of: Le village des cannibales.
Includes bibliographical references and index.
ISBN 0–674–93900–X
1. Monéys, Alain de, d. 1870—Assassination. 2. Hautefaye (France)—History.
3. Franco-Prussian War, 1870–1871—Atrocities.
4. Nobility—France—Hautefaye—Biography. I. Title.
DC280.5.M67C6713 1992
944'.72—dc20
91–33028
CIP

Contents

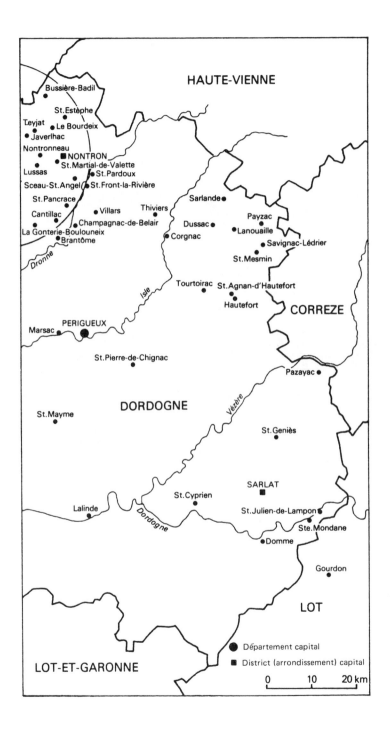

HAUTE-VIENNE

Bussière-Badil

St.Estèphe

Teyjat   Le Bourdeix

Javerlhac

Nontronneau

NONTRON

St.Martial-de-Valette

Lussas   St.Pardoux

Sceau-St.Angel   St.Front-la-Rivière

St.Pancrace

Cantillac   Villars   Thiviers   Sarlande

Champagnac-de-Belair   Payzac

La Gonterie-Boulouneix   Dussac   Lanouaille

Brantôme   Corgnac   Savignac-Lédrier

Dronne   St.Mesmin

Isle

Tourtoirac   St.Agnan-d'Hautefort

CORREZE

Hautefort

PERIGUEUX

Marsac

St.Pierre-de-Chignac

Pazayac

DORDOGNE   Vézère

St.Mayme

St.Geniès

SARLAT

St.Cyprien

Lalinde   St.Julien-de-Lampon

Dordogne   Ste.Mondane

Domme

Gourdon

LOT

● Département capital

■ District (arrondissement) capital

LOT-ET-GARONNE

0   10   20 km

The Incident

The date is August 16, 1870. The place is Hautefaye, a commune in the Nontron district *(arrondissement)* of the Dordogne *département*. On the fairground, a young noble is tortured for two hours, then burned alive (if indeed still alive) before a mob of three hundred to eight hundred people who have accused him of shouting "Vive la République!" When night falls, the frenzied crowd disperses, but not without boasting of having "roasted" a "Prussian." Some express regret at not having inflicted the same punishment on the parish priest.

The scene now shifts forward in time to February 1871. The republican journalist Charles Ponsac supplies details that turn tragedy into historical object: "Never in the annals of crime has there been so dreadful a murder. Imagine! It happened in broad daylight, in the midst of merrymaking, before a crowd of thousands *[sic]*! Think of it! This revolting crime lacked even the cover of darkness for an excuse! Dante is right to say that man sometimes exhibits a lust more hideous than concupiscence: the lust for blood."[1] Later in the article we are told that "the crime of Hautefaye is in a sense a wholly political act."

The enigma of Hautefaye, as well as its continuing fascination, lies in this tension between horror and political rationality. We must therefore turn to history, to what it was that first brought horror and politics together and then prized them apart, in order to clarify our understanding of what proved to be, in France, the last outburst of peasant rage to result in murder.

1

A Consistency of Sentiment

My purpose here is not to write the history of Périgord in the nineteenth century but to identify those ingredients constituting the alchemy—strange even to contemporaries—out of which came the cruelty of Hautefaye. Recourse to the past is necessary, not to uncover the causes of the crime (an inquiry that would be naïve, futile, and obsolete) but to understand its meaning, to penetrate the psychological mechanisms that led to murder.

The logic of the crowd's behavior has roots. The Hautefaye tragedy must remain opaque to anyone unwilling to deduce words and acts from representations of self and other. To understand the event, we must understand the history of social images of danger and, more specifically, the genealogy of what was a vague but coherent (albeit, in the eyes of contemporaries as well as historians, aberrant) vision, widely shared in rural Périgord, of a dreadful plot involving nobles, priests, republicans, and Prussians.

The impediments to such an inquiry obviously lie in the nature and origin of the sources themselves. We must be careful not simply to reproduce or to follow too closely the interpretations of contemporary observers, who were for the most part government officials. We must stick as close as we can to the actors—must keep our ears attuned to their cries as well as to their boasts, and our eyes alert for even the most insignificant of their acts.[1] The essential thing is to relive the events of August 16, 1870, when suppressed anxiety exploded into irrepressible rage that apparently nothing short of murder could quell.

The Straw and the Yoke

The peasants of southwestern France detested the nobility. This fact is well known and generally taken for granted. Yet we must try to distinguish reality from fantasy and, even more, must try to show how reality and fantasy interacted. Nineteenth-century Périgord was still a region of many castles, probably because it had been a border zone during the Hundred Years War.[2] The ubiquity of fortified châteaux played a large part in shaping the region's image. *Jacquou le Croquant,* a novel about a rebel peasant *(croquant)* from the area, was widely known. To many, Dordogne seemed a region of vast estates owned by an arrogant nobility.[3]

Thanks to Ralph Gibson, we know that the force of these stereotypes owed a great deal to the influence exerted on the popular imagination by the rural bourgeoisie, whose size and power have for too long been underestimated. This bourgeoisie achieved its greatest influence under the July Monarchy, after which it began to wither. Ultimately it would be replaced by an urban elite that promoted a different set of social images. Toward the end of the censitary monarchy (during which the right to vote and hold office was subject to property qualifications) the mayors of many villages, particularly in the Nontron district, were drawn from the ranks of the rural bourgeoisie. This social group had an interest in disguising or concealing its avarice, usury, lack of charity, sharp dealing, and mistreatment of tenant farmers.[4] Through its long battle with the nobility the bourgeoisie had obtained certain advantages, and it needed to protect these by preventing peasants from arriving at any clear understanding of their situation.

Among the tactics it employed to that end were "shrewd manipulation of age-old animosities"[5] and distortion of actual facts. The French Revolution had provoked an outpouring of antinoble rhetoric in the region, and the rural bourgeoisie seized upon, amplified, and spread this rhetoric throughout the countryside.[6] The Revolution was the source of a powerful myth, according to which the nobility's guilt stemmed not so much from its alleged social crimes as from its biological nature. This myth flourished through much of the nineteenth century and played a crucial role in the history of social representations. It may even have influenced the behavior of nobles, some of whom were tempted to behave as they imagined the nobles of the late eighteenth century had behaved.

The rural bourgeoisie hoped to focus social antagonisms away from issues of wealth and land ownership, prizes that it successfully coveted, and toward individuals and the aristocratic "caste." To that end, it exaggerated the importance of genealogy; it caricatured the pride and insolence of the noble, which were no doubt a crueler torture for the bourgeois than for the peasant; it criticized the ways in which the aristocracy strove to maintain social distance; and it sought to persuade peasants, who also hated the aristocracy, that the nobility's arrogance was the chief source of social conflict. It so happens that the rural bourgeoisie's powers of persuasion were great: the bourgeoisie "had direct contact with the peasants and enjoyed over them the influence that comes from education and wealth, an influence that was not diminished by the mistrust the aristocracy inspired in the common folk."[7]

Specifically, the rural bourgeoisie approved of, and attempted to stir up, peasant fears of a reinstatement of the nobility's former privileges. It raised the specter of a restoration of feudal rents and dues, a reinstitution of seigneurial justice, and a restitution of "national properties" (estates confiscated during the Revolution and sold to new owners). Rumors were spread to foster belief in a mythical conspiracy that would remain an obsession of the rural masses throughout the nineteenth century. The bourgeoisie denounced aristocratic emblems and other signs of distinction as intolerable: among the symbols criticized were weathervanes on castle turrets, private church pews, and *fleurs de lys* on coats of arms. The closeness of the alliance between clergy and nobility was exaggerated, exacerbating longstanding anticlerical sentiments in smallholding peasants.

The rural bourgeoisie acted on a society that was still intact, not yet plunged into disarray by rural exodus[8]—a society in which the complexity of social relations privileged intermediaries while encouraging the infiltration, transfer, and spread of unfavorable images.

The bourgeois strategy of influencing the peasantry, coupled with the autonomous workings of the peasant psychology, resulted in a representational system that bore little relation to reality. The Périgord nobility at this time was extremely heterogeneous.[9] It had been infiltrated by outsiders, who modeled their behavior on ancient codes which they revised and exaggerated. To a greater extent than the old families, these new nobles tended to fit the image of the nobility created by the Revolution. The wealth of the noble class seems, on the whole, to have been relatively modest; there were no vast estates. Under the censitary monarchy some quite "ridiculous notables" had qualified as electors, particularly in the Nontron district and despite the extensiveness of tenant farming in that tiny region.[10] The nobility of the Dordogne *département,* and particularly of its northern part, had little head for business. Few of its members showed any interest in agronomy. "The aristocracy, with its paternalistic prejudices and lack of concern for profit, exploited the peasant to only a very moderate degree."[11] And it exerted very little influence on those who tilled its land.

There were, however, limited areas, virtual islands, in which the nobility retained great power and influence. The rural bourgeoisie singled out these areas in its propaganda, a tactic that served to revive old animosities. One such area was the canton of Mareuil, near Hautefaye, which was referred to in the region as "Little Vendée" (in allusion to Vendée in western France, a locus of resistance to the Revolution). Its center was Beaussac. The murder victim Alain de Monéys, *adjoint* (deputy mayor) of the commune, belonged to this restricted group of still influential nobles, unrepresentative of the Nontron district as a whole but useful for maintaining the mythical image "of a peasantry owing fealty to a nobility reminiscent of the Ancien Régime."[12]

In fact, the nobles of Périgord, though supposedly impatient to restore prerevolutionary society and all its privileges, had kept a fairly low profile since the Revolution. Fainthearted supporters of the First Empire, they had proved discreetly rebellious during the Restoration.[13] After the revolution of July 1830, the nobility of Dordogne did actually engage in a kind of resistance: forty-two municipal officials belonging to this class refused to take an oath to support the new regime. The importance of this abstention should not be exaggerated, however. Nearly half of the mayors belonging to the aristocracy retained their positions. In 1821, nobles headed 135 communes (23 percent); the number remained as high as 62 (11 percent) in 1841 and even as late as 1861.[14] Note, moreover, that Dordogne deputies elected under the limited (censitary) suffrage of the July Monarchy adopted a moderate attitude up to the downfall of Louis-Philippe.[15]

The majority of Périgord's nobles gave their support to the Second Empire, a fact that is more directly of interest to us here. In the Nontron district only two municipal officials, both of the old nobility, refused to take the oath in 1852, and according to the subprefect *(sous-préfet)* three others had "to be considered as having refused."[16] Hence, there is almost no ground for asserting that the murder at Hautefaye was a response to open, outspoken hostility of aristocrats to the regime. In this region, however, support for the prince-president after December 1848 and later for the emperor was led by the rural bourgeoisie, which was also the principal beneficiary of the new regime.

In fact, many Périgord nobles retained legitimist sympathies despite their apparent acceptance of the new regime. The zeal with which such sympathies were noted owed much to the fact that the administration, like the bourgeoisie, needed such smoldering resistance to strengthen its hold on the peasants. Hence, the administration did nothing to advertise the nobles' support.[17] This self-serving discretion masked the reality and helped perpetuate the image of a haughty nobility nostalgic for the Ancien Régime.

At the end of the Second Empire, however, events took a paradoxical course. The rural bourgeoisie, victim of its own Malthusianism, began to decline before the nobility did.[18] Boredom with rural life, limited social contacts, fascination with the city, and concerns for their children's careers led many members of the bourgeoisie to join the exodus from the countryside. The aristocracy, meanwhile, remained more closely bound to the soil and to family traditions. It also had the means, which its bourgeois rivals lacked, to sustain an active social life far from the great towns. True, downhearted Périgord nobles tended to subscribe to an image of themselves largely derived from literary sources. Yet they did actually regain some of their former importance when their adversary the bourgeoisie collapsed. The nobility exerted considerable social influence through the distribution of charity and through its power over its domestics, tenants, and employees. And prosperity, which benefited the aristocracy along with everyone else, only increased that influence.

Périgord nobles, despite their reputation for insolent pride, seem to have displayed a certain condescension. They had no compunction, for example, about appearing at the fairground on market days. Once again, image and reality did not correspond. "Among us," the abbé Bernaret wrote the bishop of Périgueux in 1863, "the nobles have none of that cocksure air or haughty tone and manners that you see elsewhere and that make aristocrats seem as though they belong to another world. [Here] they mix with the bourgeoisie, mingle with the common people, and participate in business just like the rest."[19] Yet this familiar attitude and willingness to mingle would cost Alain de Monéys his life precisely because they were not enough to root out old animosities or counter charges of arrogance. In the Orne or Mayenne *départements,* a noble would no doubt have been content to send his steward or one of his farmers to a fair like the one at Hautefaye. The timorous nobles of Nontron, so modest in their ambitions, hardly bear comparison with the aristocrats of Mayenne, energetic builders of castles and churches who dreamed of emulating England's country nobility.[20]

Now we can understand the nature of the Dordogne peasants' hostility toward the nobility. It was a hostility that stemmed from daily contacts and experience, from bruised sensibilities. It fed on rancor that festered behind a mask of sly deference, waiting for the day when open irony would become possible.[21] It was perhaps even more a hostility inspired by an image that was first foisted on the nobility by the bourgeoisie but later embraced by the aristocrats themselves, and that also stemmed from memories endlessly reworked and reinterpreted in the course of transmission, from myths sustained by rumor, and from anxious belief in fantastic conspiracies.

For the historian the crux of the matter involves the origin, nature, and function of rumor, of which there has unfortunately been no systematic study.[22] Anyone who wishes to explore the logic of mass behavior must trace the course of rumor. Rumor reveals the social tensions that divide those who spread it. More than any other means of disseminating information, rumor gives voice to desires and anxieties. "It allows repressed emotions to appear, and exacerbates them."[23] Hence, we must pay attention to more than just the content of rumor. We must treat rumor as a source of disturbing pleasures—pleasures of expression and understanding. "Rumor brings about a consummation of social relations, a reinforcement

. . . of social bonds."[24] Rumor carries an emotional charge as it gives expression to a group's latent social mythology; so does an act like the Hautefaye murder. Between the two there is a difference of degree, not of kind.

When the peasants of Dordogne spoke among themselves of *messieurs* (gentlemen) and *habits* (fancy clothes), they were voicing an autonomous desire for liberty and equality, recasting the discourse of their "betters" in terms of their own rhetoric of fear and hatred.

Hostility took different forms in different regions. In Périgord it was focused on signs of superiority and distinction, directed more against emblems and pretensions than against individuals and property. And such had been the case since the Revolution. When châteaux were attacked in 1789 and 1790 and it became obvious that the old solidarity between nobility and people had broken down and that enmity now had the upper hand, it was the emblems of feudalism that bore the brunt of peasant wrath.[25]

It is unfortunate that there is no study of the Hundred Days in Dordogne. A link in memory's chain is missing. We know that in certain parts of southern France the "revolution of 1815" and particularly the confused period after Waterloo left deep traces.[26] There are indications that the same may have been true of Périgord. The king and the nobility had returned to France in the wagons of a foreign army—an event still in living memory in 1870; the attitude of the nobility reawakened memories of the Princes' Army and encouraged rumors of conspiracy, treason, and connivance with Prussians and Cossacks. More important still, this coalition had been formed *against the emperor.* "Our peasants," the justice of the peace of the canton of Thiviers noted in July 1851, "detest those whom they call nobles."[27] To the peasants, "this was the caste that was proscribed under the First Republic, that was accused of complicity with the foreign invasion in 1814, [and] that was *the emperor's enemy in 1815,* while working to reconstruct the Ancien Régime under royal governments."[28] The events of July 1870, which gave rise to the tragedy at Hautefaye, might have been seen as a repeat of 1815, although the Hundred Days were not explicitly mentioned.[29]

The Revolution of 1830 brought festering hatred out into the open. Emotions ran high until December, while peasants celebrated in the countryside. The mayor of Marsac, addressing his people in the local patois, declared that they no longer had to fear the "return of the tithe and rents and other dues that our fathers abolished."[30] Once again the châteaux became targets. The most serious incident occurred in Pazayac, where the mayor was slow to hoist the tricolor. Early in the afternoon on the day of the celebration, a crowd of peasants, mostly from places in nearby Corrèze, attacked the residence of the comte de Manssac, reviled for his arrogance. In the absence of the proprietor and despite the opposition of local authorities and townsmen, the orchard was ruined and the château invaded and pillaged. Linen, fat, lard, pots of jam, and spirits were carried off. The rioters deplored the absence of the Manssacs. Had it been possible to lay hands on them, their "guts [would have been] ripped out."[31]

With the fall of the July Monarchy, verbal violence against nobles resumed. Both Dordogne and nearby Basse-Marche were rife with rumor.[32] It was widely reported that "châteaux in the Mareuil region were sacked, but discrepancies between versions proved that the reports were baseless."[33] Incendiary signs went up. A column of two hundred peasants marched on the Bugeaud estate at La Durantie. But the *maréchal,* who had rallied to the republican regime, organized the defense of his property with the help of friends and tenants. The attackers were content to hurl oaths at him and then disperse. The following Sunday, the inhabitants of the commune of Lanouaille, afraid that the man they called "father" and "benefactor" might have been offended, staged a people's banquet in his honor and, singing patriotic hymns, escorted him back to La Durantie. The *maréchal,* who had donned a peasant's smock for the occasion, thanked them in patois. This episode reveals a great deal about the tactics of social control; it also shows that hatred and gratitude coexisted in the mind of the peasant, whose hostility toward local nobles was tempered by anxious need for their mediation.

Following the June insurrection in Paris, "certain residents of Pazayac dreamed of reviving the troubles of 1830."[34] It was announced in a hundred communes that the châteaux of the region would be pillaged. The comte de Manssac and several other aristocrats living in nearby castles threw up defensive fortifications.[35]

These incidents all demonstrate the importance of rumor. They highlight the contrast between the depth of the social tensions, the intensity of the anxiety, and the restraint of violence. Hatred smoldered, but a verbal venting of wrath was enough to prevent a conflagration. In order to understand what happened in Hautefaye on August 16, 1870, we must therefore pay close attention to what was said and not be misled by rhetorical excess. A note from the directorate of police of the Ministry of the Interior dated August 2, 1838, calls attention to what the writer felt was a striking contrast between the foolishness of the rumors in circulation and the numbers of people who had heard them. In Dordogne, he wrote, the most "absurd [rumors were] continually circulated and avidly received in our villages. They say that the rich will force the poor to eat straw, and that anyone who does not wear fancy clothes will soon be prohibited from keeping oxen with horns, and a thousand other things, all equally nonsensical."[36]

The yoke, a symbol of servitude, is only one of many animal metaphors that figured in these rumors. In 1849 the peasants of the Lalinde region became convinced that the marquis de Gourgues, a moderate candidate for the Legislative Assembly, kept more than a hundred yokes in his castle for hitching peasants to plows to till his land.[37]

From such perceived threats came a violent rhetoric that grew even more vehement when a weakening of governmental authority revived the specter of 1793. In June 1848 in Saint-Cyprien the curé Picon found himself the victim of popular justice. The crowd that jeered him and drove him out of town also attacked the rich, especially nobles. Emile Lasserre, known as Pontet, the mayor's brother and son of the doctor who commanded the national guard (hence a perfect symbol of the rural bourgeoisie), was alleged to have made public threats in a local club and several other places: "We shall go to the rich," he is alleged to have stated, "we shall trample them underfoot."[38] Remember this plan: it would be put into practice on the fairground at Hautefaye. Pontet allegedly added: "Down with nobles! Down with priests! . . . The Republic will not be secure in Saint-Cyprien until we have chopped off thirty heads." At the club where he was president, he allowed threats of castration to be made. Other individuals named by the prosecutor shouted, "Down with the rich! Down with nobles! Down with the band of blackguards!" and called for the guillotine. Old complaints resurfaced: nobles, according to Pierre Lasfilles, "are brigands who have seized the commune's property." Not content to have made threats of castration, Edouard Nayrat allegedly used a pick-axe to demolish buildings belonging to the Marzacs and Beaumonts. Other individuals also threatened to kill nobles.

The imperial government put an end to such verbal excess, to such joyful venting of the imagery of aggression and brutality. But officials, whom we must take at their word, reported that hatred persisted nevertheless. "Even during the peaceful days of the Second Empire, rancor against the nobility smoldered in the countryside of Périgord."[39]

Seditious Flowers

Even more virulent than hatred of the nobility was hatred of curés.[40] Ralph Gibson's work, cited earlier, shows that the rural bourgeoisie, for the time being resolutely anticlerical, liked to stir up peasant hostility against the clergy. The bourgeoisie deliberately exaggerated the closeness of the ties between clergy and nobility and charged that the two, working in league, hoped to restore the Ancien Régime.

There is little evidence for any such alliance. There is no sign in Dordogne of a correlation between size of noble estates and intensity of religious practice. By contrast, there are many signs of tension between clergy and nobility. Few aristocrats sat on vestry councils.[41] Few nobles appeared on the lists of individuals to receive Lenten letters from the bishop. No noble in the Nontron district had a domestic chapel. Unlike the noble families of western France, those of Dordogne did not make lavish gifts to the Church. Those in the canton of Mareuil gave relatively little to religious establishments. What is more, the nobility clung jealously to its children: of 1,800 priests born in the diocese and practicing there between 1830 and 1914, only 19 were aristocrats.[42] Not a single noble was ordained from 1839 to 1872. This long drought was ended the following year, when Gaston de Monéys, brother of the victim of Hautefaye, entered the priesthood.

The Nontron district was not, on the whole, a fervent region. In that respect and others, it resembled nearby Limousin. In response to an episcopal survey in 1835, 51 percent of priests in that small region reported that "superstitions" had a foothold in their parishes.[43] Hautefaye illustrates the prevailing lack of enthusiasm: only

5 percent of the men in 1855, and only 2 percent in 1863, performed their Easter duties. If the majority of women in the town still did observe those duties in 1855, their number had dropped to seventy, or 26 percent, by 1863.[44] All told, only 14 percent of those old enough to receive communion did so in the Easter season of 1863.

Still, the waxing and waning of religious fervor was as erratic here as it was in other parts of France. In the aftermath of the revolution of July 1830, religious practice appears to have subsided, although we cannot be sure that the Restoration clergy did not exaggerate the extent of earlier participation. Be that as it may, religion does appear to have scored substantial gains in the interval between two extensive surveys conducted by the bishop in 1841 and 1875. Fervor was on the rise, even in the Nontron district, although apparently not in Hautefaye, which according to the figures above resisted the general trend.

For our purposes, the crux of the matter is not lack of religious enthusiasm but "endogenous" anticlericalism in these rural populations, a factor that we shall see at work in the drama of August 16, 1870. This anticlericalism has been described too often to bear repeating here.[45] Rural people were angered by the strictness of dour priests hostile to dancing and cabarets, opposed to secularization of festivals, apt to intervene in communal affairs, and prone, it was felt, to overcharging for ceremonies. An even more contentious issue was the refusal of religious burial. Consider this example, of fairly late date: in May 1865, the curé of Saint-Julien-de-Lampon refused to bless the body of a suicide. The faithful gathered in front of the church to which the casket had been taken. In the absence of a priest, a cortège formed, preceded by a cross shrouded in black cloth. Two precentors intoned the *Miserere,* and several people carried candles. In the end the crowd agreed to stop singing only when asked to do so by the mayor and his assistant. According to the subprefect of Sarlat, the affair "left a most unfortunate impression and stirred up great discontent among the residents of the commune."[46] As in many other regions, priests were occasionally threatened with the *assouade* (being forced to mount an ass backward and be paraded through the town) and *charivaris* (raucous, sometimes obscene demonstrations), but such behavior was not typical of the region. The crucial point is that the anticlericalism of Périgord peasants focused on signs of a link between the clergy and the nobility, on suggestions of a conspiracy to restore the distinctions and privileges of the Ancien Régime.

These tensions crystallized around three issues: the removal of church pews, fees for bell ringing, and free access of parishioners to the choir portion of the church.[47] Private pews had been burned in Périgord in 1790 but were subsequently reinstituted by agreement of nobles and clergy, a restoration that offended the village communities. In 1838 anger over these issues erupted. The disturbances began on June 3 at Saint-Agnan d'Hautefort, where "a great commotion [broke out] in the church during the celebration of the Mass, the balustrade was broken, pews [were] smashed," and the tocsin was sounded. The vestry council decided that "henceforth only priests and cantors would be admitted into the church sanctuary and that no bells would be rung for baptisms and burials without payment of a fee."[48] On June 7 the mayor and other officials seeking to enforce these decisions were molested. The arrest of the troublemakers caused a hostile crowd to gather. Threatened with death, the mayor was forced to sign an order freeing the prisoners. A prefect, investigating magistrate, royal prosecutor, and general set out for Saint-Agnan, but emissaries warned of their arrival. The tocsin was sounded again. A substantial crowd, armed with clubs, pitchforks, and rifles, hurried to Saint-Agnan from surrounding villages. For a while the situation remained in stalemate.

But unrest spread throughout the region.[49] Emissaries were dispatched to Haute-Vienne and Corrèze to stir up resistance. The disturbances also involved the Nontron district. On the night of June 22, 1838, certain individuals entered the church at Dussac to ring the bells, as was customary for Saint John's Day.[50] On June 27 the tocsin was sounded at Saint-Mesmin and church pews were burned. The same things happened at Lanouaille and Dussac. At Sarlande on June 29, someone dragged all sixteen chairs from the church into the village square.[51]

On the night of July 14, new disorders broke out in Dussac, obliging the prosecutor to hasten to the scene. Forty men armed with scythes, slings, clubs, and rifles occupied the town for five to thirteen hours until the mayor signed an order freeing two troublemakers arrested the night before.[52]

Elsewhere the contentious issue was the choice of procession routes. But "in all circumstances," the prosecutor noted, "wealthy people, and particularly nobles, owners of châteaux, were the object of threats."[53] During this period, mayors and their assistants sometimes negotiated with the rioters.

Many considered the stakes to be quite high. Alarmed pew owners attached great importance to the removal of pews and chairs from church grounds. They viewed these incidents as signs of a "new jacquerie," or peasant uprising.[54] The episcopal authorities would have liked to settle the dispute by eliminating the pews but were forced to give way to aristocratic family pride. The courts, as usual in such cases, proved remarkably indulgent. The tribunal at Périgueux acquitted the four accused from Saint-Agnan. This acquittal was reversed by another court in Angoulême, but even then the sentences handed out ranged from two to six days in jail. This tradition of leniency is worth noting, for it helps explain the shock of those punished for the murder of Alain de Monéys.

In 1848 country folk again launched an attack on private pews, which were burned in some parishes. On March 8 there was a disturbance in the commune of Sourzac, and the priest and vestry council were threatened. The demonstrators won a reduction of the seating fee and an end to burial distinctions.[55]

The verbal violence that erupted during these disturbances indicates the depth of the hostility. Consider, for example, what happened to poor Picon, the curé of Saint-Cyprien, in June 1848. He was threatened with an *assouade* and "unspeakable tortures" before being expelled from the commune. Amid talk of trampling the rich underfoot or sending them to the guillotine, Emile Lasserre (Pontet) declared that "if Picon comes back, I will rinse my hands in his blood."[56] Abel Jardel also threatened to kill the unfortunate priest. Charles Fournier, known as France, "would have cut the curé to bits." Antoinette Passegand, the wife of Magimel, known as Terreyrote, and Suzon Selves, known as Teillette, planned to "mutilate curé Picon." When the authorities attempted to reinstate the banished priest on December 12, women and children armed with stones prevented them from entering the presbytery, while the men formed a menacing circle around the gendarmes. It took armed force to disperse the demonstrators.

The reader will have noticed the repeated threats of castration emanating from this population of cattle breeders, as well as the menace of physical dismemberment. Let us keep these in mind, with the full knowledge that such threats were not merely metaphorical. On January 24, 1870, seven months before the murder of Alain de Monéys, the prefect wrote to the minister of the interior: "Three young children attending the public school at Tourtoirac, some fifty kilometers from Hautefaye, were accused of attempting to castrate one of their youngest classmates, by the name of Chavoix," the same name as that of the republican candidate in the district, a man roundly disliked by the perpetrators' parents. The investigation conducted by the school inspector "established the guilt of these youths beyond any doubt . . . but also led to the revelation of a related fact: a youngster of the same age and from the same school as Chavoix allegedly attempted to castrate himself."[57] The prefect concluded: "It would appear that these facts, strange as they may seem, are not without precedent in the canton of Hautefort." Less than three months later, in the same commune of Tourtoirac, "a little girl was allegedly raped by a student monitor from the boys' school, assisted by two classmates who held the victim's arms."[58] Note that shortly before the torture inflicted on Alain de Monéys, a bourgeois observer was shocked to discover the matter-of-fact ease with which youths inflicted cruelty on the bodies of other young people.

Under the Second Empire unruly anticlericalism was obliged, along with much else, to discover restraint: the undeniable reconquest of souls by the clergy and the strict maintenance of law and order by the authorities kept violent demonstrations in check until 1868, although it is true that underlying hostility found other forms of expression. Rural municipalities vied with the presbytery for scarce state subsidies. The cost of maintaining church property took money away from plans to modernize the communal infrastructure. Protests were heard nearly everywhere, particularly in Hautefaye, about the modest livings accorded to clergymen.

Rumor, however, could not be stopped as easily as violence, and wild stories now became the only outlet for anticlerical sentiment. Nobles and "curés" were said to have fomented a plot to overthrow the emperor. When tensions boiled over, when the rumors came together and found corroboration in actual facts, people rose to defend the sovereign from threats that, once again, struck government officials as odd.

On August 21, 1862, simultaneous fires destroyed three barns and several haystacks in the communes of Saint-Martial, Pizou, and

Minzac.[59] Peasants noted uneasily the presence of "travelers of suspicious appearance." Widespread outbreaks of fire during the next few days triggered panic in the region. Area residents formed a militia to search for the arsonists. By the end of the month, peasants in Servanches, Saint-Barthélemy, and Echourgnac were "stricken with fear."[60] They had become convinced that the fires had been set deliberately by arsonists using incendiary grenades. The rumors became more specific. "There is frequent talk of a luxurious carriage said to be traveling mysteriously by night, without lights, allegedly in order to bring food and demolition devices to the arsonists." Names were named: the accusations focused on "the clerical party, which allegedly planned to sow panic among the rural population, to drive people toward fanaticism by striking at their material interests in order to make them believe in divine retribution intended to punish resistance to the pope." A smaller number of voices blamed "secret societies." Red and white stood side by side in this fantasy of threat and hatred.

In 1868 the agitation reached new heights. Haunted by the "ghost of the tithe," peasants rioted over a vast area that included Charente, Dordogne, and part of Gironde.[61] In La Rochelle the new bishop, Monsignor Thomas, despite being a liberal was still keen on displaying an imposing escutcheon engraved with his coat of arms, which contained heads of grain and daisies. Peasants became frightened when sacristans affixed the escutcheon above church doorways and inside the sanctuary, because they took the grain and flowers as symbols of a plot to overthrow the emperor and reinstate the tithe.

This belief only strengthened a movement that had begun some time earlier. As early as April there had been "tumultuous demonstrations" aimed at "ridding churches of altar flowers, the lily [symbol of the Bourbon monarchy] in particular being considered a seditious emblem."[62] On Sunday, April 18, in Cercoux, a crowd of six hundred decided to invade the church and toss out any suspect bouquets. Despite the exhortations of the mayor, several individuals entered the sanctuary and, to the applause of onlookers, snatched away the incriminated plants. "To the parish office!" cried one demonstrator, brandishing a rope. If "the curé won't hand over all the flowers in the church, we'll string him up." The mob followed his lead. The priest was forcibly detained. The demonstrators brushed aside the mayor's orders and invaded the church. A *briga-*

dier (constable) from Montguyon who attempted to stop them was attacked. "Kill the scoundrel, cut him to bits, grab him, beat him, down with the tithe!" shouted one leader. "Let's skin him alive!" added another.[63]

In the face of such threats, the *brigadier,* seeking to save his life, did what anyone would do in such a situation, and what Alain de Monéys would attempt unsuccessfully to do in Hautefaye two years later: he ran to the inn. The innkeeper hid the officer in a room on an upper floor. For three hours the menacing mob laid siege to the establishment, dispersing only at nightfall. According to the magistrates, the most hotheaded of the rioters were all good family men, longtime residents of the parish. Their previous conduct was above reproach. These men, said to be staunch supporters of Napoleon III, reportedly joined the crowd when they heard "the shout of 'Vive l'empereur!'"[64]

Late in the spring the agitation spread to Jonzac. All over the district, peasants uttered similar cries and attempted to seize the allegedly symbolic bouquets. Armed, like their successors in Hautefaye, with clubs, they gathered in large numbers along the route followed by the bishop of La Rochelle. Some took down the episcopal coat of arms; others invaded churches and attacked other hated symbols. In more than forty sanctuaries crowds damaged furniture, glass, and ornaments.[65] The disturbances then spread to Gironde, particularly in the region of Blaye. Trouble broke out in the commune of Donnezac on May 25, the day of the Perpetual Adoration.[66] The wave of unrest rolled on into Dordogne before finally subsiding in the Cognac district of Charente.[67]

A short while later, the residents of Sigogne (Charente), having returned to their senses, petitioned for a pardon to be granted to those imprisoned, whose devotion to the sovereign and the dynasty was emphasized. To justify their actions they claimed to have been victims of a "temporary and, so to speak, epidemic madness" brought on by insistent rumors and a sincere desire—which no one questioned—to serve Napoleon III.[68] The prefect of Charente and, even more emphatically, the baron Eschassériaux, a member of the Corps Législatif and the most influential figure in the *département,* recommended that a pardon be granted to mark the Festival of the Emperor (August 15). Harsh punishment, they argued, would make it difficult for the official candidates to win the upcoming elections.

Those residents of Sigogne who had been found guilty were either set free or had their already light sentences reduced by half. The courts' leniency toward the peasantry, loyal in its support of Napoleon III, was nothing new. It explains, I repeat, the shocked reaction of the men accused of the Hautefaye murder.

We have already noted the similarities between these events and the tragedy of August 16, 1870. In this affair of flowers and escutcheons, certain features are worth noting: the fanciful character of the threat, the lightning-fast spread of rumor, the certainty of a plot, the concern with decoding the sign that was supposed to initiate that plot's execution, and the helplessness of municipal authorities in the face of a determined crowd. In the minds of the region's peasants, self-defense and defense of the dynasty were indistinguishable. Both required vigilance and perspicacity. Why, in that case, fear repression? Why hesitate to use violence?

Urban anticlericalism, which stirred unrest in both Dordogne and nearby Tarn at the end of the Second Empire, is less relevant to my subject.[69] In the towns, most anticlericals belonged to the republican bourgeoisie, which was composed of members of the liberal and commercial professions and had almost no influence on the peasantry at this time. This exogenous anticlericalism—as Ralph Gibson calls it, because it came from outside rural society—stemmed from philosophical atheism, raised the banner of free thought, and set itself the task of combating obscurantism and the influence of priests over women. It was well served by the arrogant statements of the bishop of Périgueux. In all these ways this urban anticlericalism can be distinguished from the visceral hatred that racked a peasantry obsessed with images of the Ancien Régime.

Be that as it may, the outspoken hostility of urban anticlericals inevitably stirred up animosity against the church, particularly when republicans took advantage of eased restrictions to mount a skillful propaganda campaign aimed at peasants in the surrounding countryside. In 1869 Louis Mie, a lawyer and leader of Dordogne's new radical generation, published a pamphlet entitled *Théories et petits négoces de Monsieur le curé* (Monsieur the Curé's Theories and Little Deals), no doubt in the hope that the work would enhance his prestige in the countryside.[70] The pamphlet attacked the priest of Saint-Martial-de-Valette, the parish of the Nontron district's chestnut grove, for receiving illegal benefices. The priest, for example, claimed the exclusive right to sell candles, whose "price he set at a lucrative level." Mie also waxed indignant about the priest's dark traffic in "old graves." The families of the recently deceased were forced to purchase neglected old tombstones. In July 1869 the anti-clericals of Périgueux loudly protested the acquittal of a rural curé accused of having murdered his housemaid.[71] At the time, these kinds of arguments no doubt seemed more persuasive to the peasants of Dordogne than did the proposed separation of church and state.

Theft of Public Funds

It is hardly surprising that residents of rural Périgord saw the noble and the curé as threatening figures. Later, after September 4, 1870, when the republicans came to power, the government would attempt to revive these old hostilities, but by then there was no emperor to be painted as the other victim of the conspiracy.[72] In fact, following the inception of the Third Republic, the Bonapartists entered into an opportunistic, tactical alliance with nobles and curés, much as the republicans had done when they joined the so-called Union Libérale under the Empire. This realignment of antagonistic blocs is a possible source of confusion. We must be careful not to project back onto the Second Empire a modification in the system of representation that did not occur until the 1870s, for if we do we will never understand the behavior of Dordogne peasants in general and, in particular, the behavior of those who took part in the murder at Hautefaye. Those peasants saw the noble, the curé, and the republican as united in a common threat to themselves and the emperor.

This yoking together of noble, curé, and republican is at first sight rather surprising. In passing, let us note the powerful outpouring of democratic sentiments, firmly rooted in a clear perception of social antagonisms, that accompanied every social disturbance since the fall of the First Empire. How was it that hatred of the rich, evident in decade after decade, came to be associated with hatred of republicans? This is a riddle that historians have yet to resolve, and the best way to proceed is therefore to listen with a fresh ear to the rumors that circulated through the countryside.

Hatred of the rich is something we have already encountered. It was ubiquitous in rural Dordogne between 1815 and 1870. The year 1830 in particular revealed the intensity of hostility and the depth of democratic feelings. From August to December, flags were raised in nearly all rural communes, bells were rung, fires were set, the white flag and the bust of Charles X were fired upon, salvos of artillery and volleys of musket-fire were heard, liberty trees were planted, and people danced and banqueted and sang hymns to liberty along with local folk songs.[73] On September 12, two days after the bourgeois national guard in the small town of Domme erected a maypole on the market square in honor of the new regime, the leader of the democrats, a lawyer by the name of Vielmon, joined with five hundred of his supporters to erect a poplar dubbed "the poor man's maypole." More than a hundred feet tall, it towered over the church steeple. The new emblem, topped by a bellicose rooster and a tricolor flag, bore the inscription: "Long live Louis-Philippe! Liberty! Public order!" The inauguration ceremony was held at night, and people danced the farandole and shouted "Long live the poor! Down with the rich!" Napoleonic tunes were also heard.

The Revolution of 1848 provided an opportunity to repeat these demonstrations. The peasants of Dordogne, like those of Limousin, voted massively in favor of the socialist-democrats on May 13, 1849. We are therefore confronted with an important question: When did the republican join the list of hated symbols? Let us try to analyze the nature of antirepublican sentiment and trace the chronology of its rise.

To that end, let us look again at the memory of the French Revolution. The way in which representations of the past are re-worked to create new social images tells us a great deal about why attitudes resist change and why conflicts are repeated.[74] It happens that all specialists on the history of the region agree that the Great Fear of 1789 manifested itself particularly early and with particular intensity in this central southwestern part of France.[75] Moreover, the Fear left particularly deep traces. In Dordogne, according to the curé of Villars, "as late as 1860, if you asked an elderly man his age he would readily respond that he was this or that many years old *on the day of the Fear.*"[76] This memory was far more vivid than fear of the *partageux* (those who called for estates to be divided up) and the agrarian law, which historians are rather too quick to cite. In other words, mention of the Revolution in these parts elicited vague memories of outside agitators and thieves. Each new crisis revived these old anxieties.[77] This was an important and recurrent psychological mechanism.

The June 1848 insurrection in Paris triggered panic in the region. On July 20, people in the communes around Thiviers expected insurgents from the capital to arrive at any moment.[78] Outbreaks of violence were anticipated, and fears focused on vagabonds, "brigands," and arsonists. "On July 22," it was reported, "there will be an invasion of bandits" from Dordogne and Charente; they were rumored to be planning a rendezvous at the fairground in Graulges. "The gendarmes and mayor of Mareuil call for reinforcements in order to remain in control of the situation."[79] Note the geography. The tiny commune of Graulges, like Hautefaye only six miles away, sat on the border between two *départements*. It had a fairground where people could assemble in the open country, safe from the urban authorities. It therefore seemed, under the circumstances and in the minds of townsfolk, a dangerous place.

The three communes of Saint-Estèphe, Teyjat, and Le Bourdeix, all in the Nontron district, succumbed to panic: "A thousand to fifteen hundred armed men gathered at the sound of the general alarm and set out to search the woods to head off what a sudden rumor reported to be an invasion of brigands."[80] The rumor had begun when one peasant thought it might be fun to frighten the children, but the important point to note is the number of people who found the jest credible. Meanwhile, townspeople were afraid, not unjustifiably, of an attack by peasants known to be upset by the "45-centime tax." With the authorities in conflict, new hostilities helped revive old images and fears.

The following year, in the wake of the "affair of June 13,"[81] fear once again gripped the countryside. As news of events in the capital spread, the Nontron district once more succumbed to panic. Clearly this border region was particularly attuned to frightening rumors. This time the mechanisms of the Great Fear were of lesser importance, and there was heightened awareness of social conflicts thanks no doubt to the work of the socialist-democrats. Ledru-Rollin reportedly had many friends in the region, and this worried the authorities. Townspeople again feared attack by armed peasants, peasants known to have voted the month before in large numbers for the "reds." Word spread that the rioters planned to assemble in the town of Corgnac.[82] The disturbances of the previous year had taught townsfolk to fear the violence of the countryside. This fear would resurface twenty-one years later in the wake of the murder at Hautefaye. But champions of law and order in the towns had little understanding of the present state of rural sentiment. The peasant agitation of the previous few months had been triggered by the so-called 45-centime tax, not by any desire to defend Ledru-Rollin and his confederates.[83]

Resentment of taxes was the true source of peasant antirepublicanism. The 45-centime tax had dismayed people in the countryside and dampened initial enthusiasm for the Second Republic, which peasants had rashly assumed meant liberation from all their burdens. This crucial episode is worth exploring in greater detail. There was in fact a long tradition of rural anticipation of tax relief.[84] Rumors flew fast and furious, and it is important to note how people envisioned the flow of cash and who they thought profited from their suffering.

In rural Dordogne in the spring of 1848, economic crisis compounded by political upheaval triggered fears shaped in part by painful memories of the Revolution. The widespread circulation of paper issued by banks and discounters revived the specter of a devalued paper currency. Peasants declined to accept what they called "the *assignats* of the new Republic" in payment for their crops. [The *assignat* was a form of government paper issued during the French Revolution.—*Trans.*] At the Nontron market, sellers offered discounts to buyers who paid hard cash.

Even more important, antitax agitation had resumed in the region in early March. Years before, in 1814 and again in 1830, in the aftermath of the July revolution, peasants had launched attacks on tax collectors.[85] At the time it was widely rumored in rural areas that one could get away with refusing to pay taxes because the new regime seemed so unstable. Anyone who paid too quickly, the story went, risked losing his money. The word was that Charles X had yet to leave France or that he would soon return at the head of foreign troops.[86]

In particular, people refused to pay the temporarily suspended tax on wine to the so-called *rats de cave,* or "cellar rats," charged with collecting it. On August 8, 1830, employees of the Verteillac excise office happened to arrive at Saint-Victor in the midst of

Patron's Day festivities and were attacked by a mob of more than three hundred people wielding clubs. The unfortunate officials had been paraded about town to shouts of "Away with all cellar rats! Kill them!" At the tavern the revenuers were forced to drink toasts with the rioters. Before being released, the captives were forced to pay a tax of six francs, later raised to twelve.[87] Death threats of this sort, which would resound through Hautefaye for hours on August 16, 1870, were common in the countryside; but before the Monéys murder, peasants had never acted on these threats, except in the heat of a village brawl. During the summer and autumn of 1830, there were other incidents: in Montagrier and Montpon, where mobs burned tax records, and later in Mussidan and Neuvic. In the Nontron district there was talk of a genuine insurrection.

But to get back to the events of 1848, many peasants began refusing to pay taxes soon after the new regime took power. Turning over additional funds to the government ran counter to their idea of republican freedom. Tax collectors were threatened. Seditious placards lumped them together with nobles and priests bent on keeping private pews in the churches. As we saw earlier, on March 7 and 8 the curé of Sourzac and his parish council were forced to agree to a reduction in the pew fee and an abolition of funeral distinctions. At the same time, tax assessors were besieged with demands to reduce taxes and eliminate license fees. They, too, received threats and insults.[88]

Early in March, disturbances broke out in several places. In Payzac taxpayers protested against early tax collections. The commander of the national guard called for tax rolls to be turned over to him so they could be burned. When the tax collector refused to hand over the documents, he was attacked with stones. Gendarmes had to be called in to restore order.

For a long time thereafter, hope alternated with disappointment. Peasants remained quite angry. They complained bitterly that the 45-centime levy ate up their savings. In Lanouaille, as we have seen, rioters marched on La Durantie, where they hoped to lay hands on the 35 million francs that Bugeaud was rumored to have stolen. It was seen as an outrage that the Republic did not force the profiteers who had fattened themselves on the fallen regime to cough up what they had taken. In late April, hopes rose with expectation of action by the Constituent Assembly. Peasants told one another that the deputies would soon abolish the 45-centime tax. Many communes, including Hautefaye, submitted petitions urging them to do so. Mayors, whether out of conviction or out of fear for their safety, refused to aid hapless tax collectors.

Hence, there was great disappointment at the end of May, when the assembly approved the tax. Rumblings of rebellion were widespread. On June 4, the day of additional special elections, rebels at Saint-Pierre-de-Chignac erected a gallows with two arms, which they mockingly called a liberty tree.[89] "Nouguier, known as Baragouin, called upon the curé to bless the device. The priest refused, on the grounds that it was an instrument of death." This parody of the Republic's primary symbol shows how disappointed the peasants were and how quickly they turned away from the new regime. The rioters flew a black flag from the gallows and attached a rope with a hook to each arm. A sign warned that anyone who paid the 45-centime tax, as well as anyone who refused to apprehend and execute such overzealous taxpayers, would be "placed in irons and hanged"; the same threats would be made against Alain de Monéys on August 16, 1870. The unanimity and solidarity of the village community were here being called into play. Such threats, common in times of riot, would be issued on the day of the Hautefaye murder.

The government prosecutor, assisted by gendarmes, ordered the gallows destroyed and made four arrests. The peasants of the region then alleged that, because of the terror to which they were being subjected, they would not pay their taxes. Attempting to assert and seize liberties of which they had long dreamed, they embarked on a variety of illegal activities. Compulsory labor services *(corvées)* were refused. Tavernkeepers stopped paying the beverage excise. Hunters took game wherever they pleased, without permits. On August 20 the gendarmes of Saint-Mayme attempted to arrest some poachers.[90] As the news spread throughout the countryside, a group of hunters assembled, surrounded the gendarmes, and threatened them with clubs, picks, stones. Reinforcements had to be called in from Bergerac before thirteen of the troublemakers could be taken into custody.

On September 3 the Constituent Assembly gave final approval to the 45-centime tax. Resistance stiffened. Tax collectors were beaten. When property was seized in lieu of taxes, no buyers appeared, so that the government was forced to give up using seizure as an enforcement tactic. Troops and gendarmes were called in, to no avail.[91] In the northern part of the *département,* despite the zealous efforts of gendarmes from Mareuil and Nontron, the peasants refused to pay. Mayors billeted soldiers on those who had paid. On December 2, at La Gonterie-Boulouneix, not far from Hautefaye, a bailiff attempting to dun several peasants for payment of debts was greeted with shouts of "Fire! Brigands! Thieves!"[92] Their cries brought neighbors running and reawakened memories of the Great Fear. The bailiff was obliged to run for his life.

The candidacy of Louis-Napoleon Bonaparte rekindled hopes. Peasants believed that he would do away with the 45-centime tax. Rumors flew: "Bonaparte," peasants had been saying since late spring, "will be emperor. He will take 400,000 men and go to England to force Louis-Philippe to pay the tax."[93] In December another rumor began making the rounds: "Napoleon is a millionaire a thousand times over. If he becomes president, he will pay France's debts and the notorious 45-centime tax."[94] Thus, a Bonapartism that was at once popular and antirepublican began to take shape. Well before the socialist-democrats borrowed the tactic, the Bonapartists encouraged peasant hopes by promising to satisfy their desires. December 10, the day of the presidential election, was a holiday throughout Périgord. The electors of Mareuil went joyfully to the polls, their ballots pinned to their hats.[95] Louis-Napoleon Bonaparte received 92,534 votes in the *département,* Cavaignac 5,259. On February 9, 1849, the four individuals indicted after the disturbances at Saint-Pierre-de-Chignac were acquitted. The courts' lenience toward the rioters heightened their confidence and stiffened their resistance.

The government, however, had no intention of altering its course. On January 23, a few days after riots in Gourdon, one of the subprefectures of Lot (the *département* adjoining Dordogne), the army intervened in Mareuil, less than ten miles from Hautefaye.[96] For two months, troops roamed the countryside of the Nontron district, ferreting out insurgents. In the northern part of the *département,* the army became at this time the symbol of the Republic.

In this affair of the 45 centimes, Dordogne was not the scene of the most serious disturbances. These took place at Ajain (Creuse) and at Gourdon (Lot).[97] We must be careful, however, not to under-estimate the magnitude of the movement in Périgord. In the Nontron district, in particular, sporadic outbreaks continued from March 1848 to February 1849. This lasting conflict not only gave evidence of but also deepened hostility to the Republic.

In the spring a new glimmer of hope appeared. The "reds" took up demands that peasants had been pressing on their own for more than a year. The socialist-democrats raised the specter of a reinstate-ment of the tithe, compulsory labor services, and feudal dues and privileges. They proposed reducing or even eliminating taxes on salt, beverages, and wagons. Above all, they called for reimbursement of the 45 centimes by way of restitution of the *milliard des émigrés* [compensation paid to repatriated émigré nobles for estates con-fiscated during the Revolution—*Trans.*]. One of Dordogne's repre-sentatives, Jean-Baptiste Chavoix, had disseminated throughout the countryside a bill he had filed to that effect and published in the *Moniteur* on April 13, 1849.[98]

The socialist-democrats thus captured the hopes of the peasants. They succeeded in convincing numerous municipal councillors from rural communes. Now, as the *procureur général* reported, "the peasants here allow themselves to be led about by the mayors, whom they regard as agents of the government."[99] Peasant electors hated the Republic of moderates, which sent out its mobile troops. In May, huge numbers of peasants swelled the socialist-democrat rolls, and the "red" candidates won by more than 16,000 votes. In Saint-Félix, national-guard units from rural communes refused to allow the polling place to be guarded by units from the town, for the latter were said to be the tools of the rich. A captain was stabbed. On May 18, peasants armed with clubs, pitchforks, and rifles gathered to prevent the arrest of their leaders. Old patterns of behavior were integrated into new political struggles.

The success of the socialist-democrats on May 13, 1849, in no way contradicts that of Louis-Napoleon Bonaparte on December 10, 1848.[100] In both cases rural voters in Périgord were looking for the same benefits. Had the socialist-democrat *montagnards* suc-ceeded in their purpose, they might have retained control over the peasants of Dordogne; but they failed. Despite the efforts of Chavoix, Pierre Leroux, Ledru-Rollin, and, later, Flocon, the Legis-lative Assembly refused to rescind its decision on the 45 centimes.

Reimbursement, even in payments spread out over some time, was ruled out.[101]

Worse, the parliamentary indemnity of 25 francs helped to discredit the representatives, who in this part of the country were now the "reds." The political attitudes of country folk were shaped by simple but urgent problems, which drew all their attention and sapped all their energy. The issues involved were quite narrow and turned on the expectation of immediate benefits. What distinguished the educated bourgeois from the peasants was not so much the logic of their arguments or the intensity of their convictions but their differing priorities and estimates of the time required for reform.[102]

There were persistent rumors about where all the money was going. The "25 francs" probably meant more to the peasants than to workers in Paris's Faubourg Saint-Antoine, who berated the deputy Baudin over the issue on December 3, 1851.[103] Twenty-five francs was ten times a farm worker's daily wage for the harvest season. That such a sum should be handed out to 750 representatives struck peasants as an enormous expenditure: it was enough to pay more than 10,000 workers in ordinary times. The costs involved in the exercise of power made a great impression on rural voters. All things considered, would it not be better to keep a single sovereign than to pay hundreds? When a teacher asked rioters in Ajain why they preferred Louis-Philippe to the Republic, their answer was couched in the form of a colorful local proverb: "Better to fatten one pig than feed five."[104]

The expenditure seemed all the more unconscionable in that it was associated with the levy of the special tax. In the rural mind, the 45 centimes and the 25 francs were inseparable. On March 22, 1852, the day after elections to the Corps Législatif, the subprefect of Nontron had this to say about the overwhelming success of the prince-president's candidate: "Our peasants asked only two questions before making up their minds to vote for him: 'Is he for Napoleon? Will he be paid?'"[105] The subprefect saw in this latter concern a manifestation "of the disgust [the peasants] had often demonstrated [note the past tense] with the 750, who received 25 francs per day for being hostile to Louis Napoleon."

The peasants were aware, moreover, that the president was not responsible for the 45-centime tax. He was, however, credited with having decreased the salt tax. Above all, there was confidence in his ability to manage things in the future. With Napoleon, country folk said, there was nothing to fear in the way of *assignats* and bankruptcy.

In other words, hatred of the rich, vague democratic feelings, support for the "reds" in 1849, and all that the red deputies had done were not enough to erase from the mind of the peasant of the Nontron district the image of a spendthrift Republic prepared to lavish funds on its leaders but quick to squeeze and discipline those who tilled the earth.

Among the peasants favorably disposed to the socialist-democrats in 1849, those who had been most vigorously opposed to the special tax had accepted Napoleon's coup d'état almost impassively.[106] Attitudes in Périgord, Quercy, and Limousin were similar. I reported these findings in an earlier work, but what I failed to notice then, owing to my failure to attend carefully, and without preconceptions, to what people did and said, was the logic of the peasants' position. Twenty-five years later, I return to the peasants of my youth (or at any rate to their traces in the archives) with, I hope, deeper insight and fuller understanding.

By reestablishing universal suffrage[107] and dismissing the 750 recipients (both red and white) of the 25 francs, Louis-Napoleon answered the prayers of the majority of Périgord's peasants. The results of the plebiscite of December 20, 1851, suggest the magnitude of his support: 112,784 votes in favor, 5,720 opposed. A total of 424 additional ballots was declared invalid because they were decorated with eagles, hats, or pro-imperial slogans. In the Nontron district, satisfaction with the coup was still more overwhelming. In Hautefaye as well as certain communes in the mountains of Limousin, all the ballots were marked "yes."

We know, however, that government officials exerted considerable pressure on the voters, and we must take this into account in attempting to evaluate the attitude of the population. Celebration of the outcome of the election is therefore more significant than the act of voting. When the results were posted, people in the villages raised flags, fired salvos, illuminated lights, organized banquets, and sent up fireworks. In some places, liberty trees that had been the butt of ridicule in the spring of 1848 were now cut down. Meanwhile, one of the largest insurrections of the century was unfolding over much of the territory.[108] The voters of central southwestern France, most of whom had supported the socialist-democrats in 1849, now jubilantly demonstrated their support for Louis-Napoleon. They showed, in fact, an ardor unprecedented except perhaps in 1830, when the Bourbons were dethroned. Despite the lapse of more than twenty years, these two outpourings of popular joy are clearly connected. They constitute two acts of retribution against the royalist restoration of 1815. For the peasants of the Nontron district, it seems, the eighteen years of the July Monarchy and, to a lesser degree, the first months of the Second Republic were nothing more than a hiatus of negligible political significance.[109]

To have said "no" to Louis-Napoleon would have been to reopen the gates "to despoilers of the public treasury": this was apparently the dominant argument in rural Périgord in December 1851. Prefect Albert de Calvimont stressed the point in a proclamation to the voters of his *département*.[110] Around this time, it was proposed that the president be given a symbolic golden broom, although we do not know how this idea found its way into Périgord. In any case, it pleased Napoleon enough that he was careful to mention it in the presence of deputies from Dordogne.

The hostility of Périgord peasants toward the republicans resurfaced in 1870. At the end of Napoleon's reign, the republican party was reborn and former *quarante-huitards* ("forty-eighters") once again asserted their authority.[111] But to the peasants it seemed that their old enemies had regained control; hence, there was no reason why they should not resume their old hostility. It was soon clear that the new generation of republican leaders was cut off from the rural electorate, as a careful reading of documents concerning the 1869 campaign shows.[112] Although republicans were allowed a relatively free hand to organize meetings in rural Dordogne, they were unable to do so. Their few attempts ended in failure. Outside the cities where their supporters lived, they were able to attract only a handful of voters, mostly artisans.[113] In the countryside, the urban bourgeoisie lacked the influence once wielded by its rural counterpart, which had organized support for Louis-Napoleon. Urban republicans did not reap the benefit of geographic and social proximity to the peasant, nor did they speak in familiar terms with which country folk could identify. The knowledge, talent, and rhetoric of this urban bourgeoisie, exemplified by attorney Louis Mie, failed to attract the peasant, at least for the time being. Republican activists were well aware of the situation and discussed it candidly, particularly after their crushing defeat in the plebiscite of May 8, 1870.[114]

In the countryside of Périgord and the district of Saint-Yriex that bordered the region on the north, support for the emperor increased between January and May 1870.[115] Rural people in the area reacted indignantly to unrest in Paris, where the emperor had been subjected to withering ridicule. People again said that it was up to the peasantry to save the Empire, and there were renewed calls to defend Napoleon III against criticism and violence. Unrest in the early months of 1870 tended to bring together long disunited fragments of the old party of order.[116] Meanwhile, rural anxiety and irritation revived old antagonisms toward the city.[117] It is difficult to understand either the results of the National Assembly election of February 8, 1871, or rural attitudes during the time of the Paris Commune without paying careful attention to what was going on in the hinterland between January and May 1870—but that is not part of our story.

The Logic of Devotion to the Emperor

Thus, there was a logic to the peasant's animosity toward priest, noble, and republican. But what about his support for the emperor? The peasant's devotion to his sovereign released emotions of great intensity, and it was this intensity that gave consistency and force to his political attitudes. I use the word "devotion" because the feelings involved went beyond mere political support. Those feelings were a fundamental part of each peasant's self-image and hence of the image of the peasantry as a group.[118] The election of December 10, 1848, the three plebiscites, and the elections to the Corps Législatif enabled rural voters to demonstrate their support for their sovereign and thus to deepen their awareness of their own political identity.

This is not the place to attempt a "genealogy" of imperial devotion, despite the fact that republicans themselves blamed it for the Hautefaye murder. There are excellent studies of the "Napoleonic legend"—its content, chronology, and means of elaboration and diffusion. We know little, however, about the emotional response the legend evoked. To that end, it is useful to study the role of rumor in the process of adhesion. What is generally called "Bonapartism" depended, in southwestern France, on peasants' becoming aware of their own identity. The exchange of information that government officials considered absurd nevertheless fostered a sense of solidarity in the peasantry. Although we know a great deal about Bonapartism in its primary manifestations, we know comparatively little about "the Empire in the village." Since the tragedy at Hautefaye depends on understanding the imperial phenomenon at the local level, it is worth pausing a moment to attempt a quick survey.[119]

The Dordogne peasant's devotion to the person of Napoleon III stemmed from his memory of the Empire's glorious past, couched in the form of the Napoleonic legend, whose effects took considerable time to make themselves felt in the countryside. For our purposes, the phenomenon of greatest interest is the slow but steady development of the myth of a Napoleon (or Napoleons) of the people.[120] These myths cast the Consulate, Empire, and, to an even greater extent, the Hundred Days as continuations of the Revolution and, more particularly, of 1793, and they cast the imperial army as the matrix of the French nation.[121]

Most of the seditious protest, most of the demonstrations of hatred or insolence toward the king and the royal family during the Restoration, stemmed from nostalgia for the Empire.[122] When the monarchy fell in 1830, joyous celebrations erupted throughout rural Dordogne, creating an air of something almost like an imperial restoration. Peasants sang imperial songs. Tricolor flags were brought down from attics for the occasion and flown by the national guards, but they were not the flags of 1789: they were "sacred relics" of the Grand Army.[123] Dubernard de Montmège, *adjoint* of Saint-Geniès, turned over to his communal section a banner he had piously preserved since Napoleon's downfall. Barrière, at one time a non-commissioned officer in the imperial army, gave the national guard of Sarlat a flag he had brought back from the campaign of 1814. And Georges Rocal wondered, with good reason, whether the eagles had been removed from the staffs to which these flags were attached.

By mid-spring of 1848, Bonapartist propaganda was bending the Napoleonic legend to its own purposes. Songs, pamphlets, engravings, and sculpture all attempted to associate the nephew with the uncle. Somewhat later, according to historians, the forces of popular democracy in Périgord were captured by agents of "Caesarism."[124] I have attempted to shed light on one aspect of this process, but it is important to understand what is implicit in this image of a "capture." It implies that a current of popular democratic feeling existed independent of the imperial idea and the emotions that infused it, and it tends to minimize the autonomy of the devotion to Bonaparte. One might equally well, and perhaps with greater justification, speak here of a *resurgence* of Bonapartism. We thus come face to face with democratic Caesarism, a phenomenon without which the political history of the nineteenth century (to 1870) must remain totally incomprehensible to anyone unwilling to reduce that history to the ideological debates conducted on the podium of the Palais Bourbon and in the salons and newspaper offices of Paris.[125]

The next stage in the process is the most important for our story: the completion of the transfer of the uncle's prestige to the nephew and the development of an unshakable devotion to the person of Napoleon III. We must be wary of anachronism and of the distorting effects of the negative myth fostered by prominent exiles during the Second Empire, reworked by late-imperial radicals, and then popularized in the early years of the Third Republic.[126] The immense success of such works as Victor Hugo's *Châtiments* and *Napoléon le Petit* can all too easily obscure the actual political sentiments of Second Empire peasants. The opposition forged its own system of representations, but the images on which that system was based were known to relatively few people. Rural folk did not learn of them until much later, in the wake of deliberate efforts to reeducate the peasantry.

For the time being, the peasants of the Nontron district felt nothing but devotion, admiration, and gratitude toward Napoleon III. These feelings gave rise to a veritable cult of the emperor, a cult that Dordogne republicans vehemently denounced at the inception of the Third Republic.[127] Louis Mie, who became the attorney for the Hautefaye murderers, based his defense on the strength of the peasants' devotion to Napoleon. But this fact should be interpreted with caution. Paradoxically, republicans found it advantageous to exaggerate the strength of peasant devotion to Napoleon III, the better to hold it up to ridicule. To hear the republicans tell it, these backward peasants actually believed in something called "imperial Providence." They literally believed that the emperor could make the rain fall and the sun shine. And they were convinced of Napoleon's invincibility, not to say immortality. Clearly these allegations are exaggerated, and just as clearly their intent is to persuade us that peasant beliefs were primitive and above all *irrational,* the better to discredit them.

What was peasant devotion to the emperor really like? We have already witnessed its powerful effect on election day, December 10, 1848, a day of reveling and drinking in the inns of Périgord.[128] Celebration erupted again on the night of December 22, 1851, and even more enthusiastically in November 1852, when results of the plebiscite on reestablishing the Empire were made public. Despite torrential rains, which swelled rivers and hampered travel during the two days of voting, only 4,936 voters abstained in the Nontron district; 19,430 voted "yes," and only 88 voted "no." In the cities many "reds" refused to vote, but according to the subprefect many of those in the countryside gave their votes to the future emperor.[129] The rift in socialist-democrat ranks had been growing wider for a year and remained all but unbreachable until the end of the regime. Opponents of the yes-vote once again attempted to turn rumor to their advantage, but to no avail. They put out the word that the new emperor would reinstate the salt tax, double the salary of priests, and increase his own remuneration under the civil list, and they insisted that he was already plotting to reestablish the indemnity paid to members of the Corps Législatif. Peasants did not believe these rumors, presumably because they failed to gratify psychological needs and hence yielded no pleasure. The false reports therefore proved of no avail in stemming the groundswell of support for Napoleon.

In the commune of Monfaucon every voter who took part in the election, 127 of the 157 registered, voted "yes." On the night of November 22, 1852, the mayor wrote to the prefect: "The magic name 'Empire' has given strength even to the most infirm, to those who had long since ceased to come to the polls."[130] Thus, even before the Second Republic had fallen, the "imperial feast" had begun to be celebrated in villages that had had virtually nothing else to celebrate politically since the spring of 1848.[131]

Encouragement from the rural bourgeoisie further strengthened support for the emperor. Unlike their urban counterparts, the rural bourgeois knew how to capitalize on peasant hostility toward the nobles. It was intimated that loud celebration of Napoleon's victory would be taken as a challenge to the power of noble and curé.

But devotion to the emperor was more than that, and it was different in December 1852—less rational than it would be in August 1870. Loyalty, it is too often forgotten, eventually creates its own justification. As time went by, memory of old fears faded and people grew less anxious about the possibility of civil unrest. Peasants interpreted these changes as justification of their devotion to the emperor and as a refutation of his, and their, enemies. The tragedy at Hautefaye was one consequence of this change in the nature of the emperor's support.

Consider the situation in the early summer of 1870. By then, peasants clearly perceived that for the previous eighteen years politics had revolved around certain "material interests." Government officials, obsessed with efficiency and progress, repeatedly professed impatience with rhetoric; their only interest, they said, was to find solutions to concrete problems, and they made a convincing case.

In making that case, officials spoke the language of modernization. For two decades they expressed concern for "the previously neglected interests of the rural population" and offered their help.[132] Peasants, who according to one prefect had no interest in anything beyond "administrative issues" of direct importance to themselves, were perfectly capable of assessing the visible and immediate effects of government action.[133]

Proponents of the new regime rejected ideology, rhetoric, and party politics as matters of base passion and instinct. Their opponents, they said, were "demagogues" motivated by zealotry, disruptiveness, jealousy, envy, vengeance, and greed. According to this "imperial" view, politics was a branch of ethics. The opposition was characterized as evil, whereas the emperor was interested in establishing a moral order. Long before the presidency of MacMahon and the government of the duc de Broglie, the phrase "moral order" began to appear with some frequency in prefects' and prosecutors' reports.[134] The government's very visible effort to develop the schools stemmed in part from its open wish to protect society from the deleterious effects of "demagogic" passions.[135]

Liberals and republicans were clamoring for "necessary freedoms."[136] What could such a phrase have meant to the peasants of

Hautefaye? Freedom of the press? This was apparently not a high priority among peasants, even those who could read (or could have someone read to them) the crime stories, advertisements, and local news that rural papers printed. Freedom of assembly? Peasants allegedly saw this as threatening a renewal of civil disturbances.

What did concern the peasant was an entirely different set of desires: striking a proper balance between, on the one hand, hunting, fishing, and passing time in the local cabaret and, on the other hand, keeping order in the countryside by ensuring that rural wardens made their necessary rounds. And order seems to have been achieved in the Nontron district, at least to judge by the triumphant reports submitted by the cantonal commissioners.[137] The peasant, it was said repeatedly, was concerned with whatever would enhance prosperity, increase production, and facilitate the transport and sale of his products. In the Nontron district, extensive work was done on local roads, and, to the dismay of some prominent citizens, fairs and markets were encouraged. Rising livestock prices led to increased peasant incomes in 1867[138] and even in the difficult year 1868.[139] As Louis Mie would point out, the peasants of Hautefaye had never been as prosperous as they were during the Second Empire.

Farmers, we are told, wanted their communes to prosper and therefore urged municipal officials to concern themselves with modernization. The years of the Second Empire in the rural Nontron district were a time of marked change, of what has been called "economic takeoff," marked by the construction of schools, the building of presbyteries, the opening of new cemeteries, and the clearing of new roads.[140]

Last but not least, peasants were proud of anything that enhanced the prestige of rural society. The regime established the first agricultural society *(comice)* in the Nontron district and sponsored innumerable village festivals.[141] On August 15, fireworks and dances augmented the pleasures of the fair.

In the political realm, as we have seen, peasants were pleased with the government's selection of mayors and with the frequent exclusion of local notables. Peasants liked being able to vote for their municipal councillors, chosen by universal suffrage. Nationally, peasants participated in the election of the Corps Législatif. They felt that they were participating in a sort of exchange with the sovereign. They gave the emperor their votes, and in return they expected solicitude, generosity, and possibly concrete rewards. Now we can see what it meant to vote for the government's officially designated candidate. To cast such a vote was not so much to elect a representative as to offer one's support to the sovereign and his dynasty. The ballot box was only one means of doing so. Others included keeping an eye out for the emperor's enemies and, in case of serious danger, coming to his defense.

It mattered little that Napoleon III's candidates were men like Magne or Welles de Lavalette. Magne, minister of finance and public works, spruced up Périgueux; the high visibility of his projects redounded to his benefit. As for Welles de Lavalette, it adds spice to our saga to discover that the "cannibals," the "primitives," of Hautefaye were for years in the habit of electing a Bostonian, a pure representative of cosmopolitan capitalism and aggressive modernity and a man who, in the eyes of many adversaries, stood as the symbol par excellence of the hated regime.

The peasant's final political concern, once security against the depredations of nobleman and priest was assured, was to see to it that military service could be avoided either through exemption or replacement. If need be, the peasant wanted to have the option of keeping his son at home by purchasing the services of a substitute soldier, a *cochon vendu* (literally, a "bought pig"—peasants were fond of animal metaphors). The drafting of a new military law preoccupied the region for a time, but anxiety never rose to the heights it attained in the region of Toulouse.[142] In Dordogne, according to officials, the worry soon passed. The idea of a mobile national guard gained quick acceptance.[143] Confidence in the emperor's military genius was such that no one imagined this force would ever be used. After all, "Pouléoun" (Napoleon) had already beaten the Russians and the Austrians, and he was a friend of England, the only power that had proved capable of standing up to his uncle. As for the fixed national guard, if units really were organized they would provide an opportunity for villagers to demonstrate their virility. Remember, too, that Napoleon III had preserved and even restored the national honor. The rural communes of the region noisily celebrated the French victory in the Crimea and successes in the war in Italy.[144]

The prestige of the sovereign was reinforced by a shrewd staging of his power and private life, and in particular by the magnificent style in which he traveled. The emperor passed through southwestern France several times on his way to Bordeaux and Biarritz. He was honored by public celebrations, larger and more numerous than in the past and accompanied by cries of "Vive l'Empereur! Vive l'Impératrice! Vive le Prince impérial!" shouted by thousands of voices. For the peasants of Dordogne, acclamation seems to have become a habit.

In times of crisis, this devotion to the emperor was displayed with greater intensity than ever. As early as 1859 there were fears in the region that an incautiously bold emperor might unwisely expose his person on the battlefields of Italy. As the emperor grew older, there were concerns for the future of the dynasty. In 1867 it was anxiously rumored in rural Dordogne that the imperial prince had come down with an incurable disease. In 1868, as we saw earlier, large crowds rallied in support of the emperor on the news that a conspiracy against him by priests and nobles was about to be put into action. Early in 1870 there were worries about the threat to the emperor from republican agitation. There was general agreement on the need to keep a wary eye out and, if need be, to rally to the emperor's defense.[145] Collective watchfulness was of the essence. Everyone had to be on the alert, and the best way to thwart conspiracy was to ensure quick dissemination of news of any threat. In fact, treason posed the only real danger to a sovereign whose defeat would also mean the defeat of the peasantry, not to say of the nation as a whole. If, as in 1868, an emergency called for immediate action, the emperor in due course would surely find a way to reward those who stood by him. In defending Napoleon III, the peasants of Dordogne felt they were championing their own cause.

The Hautefaye tragedy was not the result of any rearing up of primitive forces. Its objectives and procedures, not to say its excesses, had been shaped by previous events. The disastrous war news and the frightening new figure of the Prussian crystallized all the hostile images in the political repertoire. The social threat merged with the national threat. The extraordinary intensity of the psychological crisis led to a search for a scapegoat, a butt for all hostility. In the event, that scapegoat turned out to be a noble. It might equally well have been a priest—it almost was. It might have been a republican—as those involved believed the victim was. And of course it might have been a Prussian.

This hostile alliance—of nobles, priests, republicans, and Prussians—was a firm reality in the peasant mind. That is why the source of the threat could so easily change from one quarter to another. Without such a belief, the Hautefaye murder would be incomprehensible. The event is impervious to political science. Alain de Monéys died because he failed to grasp this basic fact. His fate was sealed in the first few minutes, in the clash of two logics, two political cultures. Scarcely had he entered the village when Brethenoux, a hawker, informed him that Monéys' cousin Camille de Maillard, a young legitimist noble, had been seized while shouting "Vive la République!" Monéys, struck by the obvious illogicality of his cousin's alleged behavior, replied that it was impossible. And that is why he died: he did not understand that, to the hundreds of peasants gathered on the fairground, it seemed only too logical that a hated member of the noble caste should be a champion of the Republic. Brethenoux immediately called for a show of hands: *all* the peasants gathered on the fairground raised their hands to signify that Camille de Maillard had indeed cried "Vive la République!" Surely he had not, but the facts are of relatively little importance.[146] At the same time, Monéys's steadfast denials, confirmed by his political logic, aroused the suspicion of the crowd. Surely he, too, was part of the conspiracy. Hence, he had to be killed for the sake of the emperor, the nation, and the killers themselves.

Before exploring this drama further, however, let us examine the circumstances more fully and set the scene of the crime.

2

Anxiety and Rumor

Prussian Cash

The Hautefaye tragedy was the result of a collective psychosis whose severity and scope we must attempt to measure.[1] According to the prefect, the people of Dordogne were not surprised by the declaration of war.[2] Since 1866, he maintained, they had considered it to be both inevitable and imminent.[3] During the first days of the war, the people of France, on the whole resigned to the conflict, displayed not eagerness for battle but "patriotic determination."[4] The departure of the troops was not marked by clamorous demonstrations like those that greeted the outbreak of World War I. By the end of July 1870, however, opinion had begun to shift. As the days passed, nationalist sentiment grew stronger, at any rate according to Stéphane Audoin-Rouzeau. The war, which had been the emperor's war, gradually became the nation's war. Perhaps that was what the prefect of Dordogne meant when he wrote of "enthusiasm" on August 6.

This "patriotic conversion" of public opinion forced the political parties to accept a government of national emergency. Opponents of the regime appeared to offer their support. To do otherwise was to risk being branded a "Prussian." Meanwhile, the highly over-touted French victory at Saarbrücken silenced even the most hostile critics of the fighting. On August 6, Dordogne celebrated this barren triumph. For a time the clergy seemed to put its grievances aside. Not even the announcement of the French garrison's withdrawal from Rome could thwart the clergy's apparent embrace of the imperial cause. In Tarn[5] and Lot[6] priests took up collections for the wounded and said prayers for the troops. Elsewhere, in Vienne for example, the clergy was more reserved, adopting an attitude of benevolent neutrality. Legitimists had greater misgivings. As of late July, the legitimist camp was actually divided. In parts of the west and southwest, legitimists sought refuge from the outburst of patriotic fervor. Moderate republicans, meanwhile, held their longstanding bitterness toward the regime in check, deferring their hopes to some unspecified future date.

The extreme left was alone, therefore, in loudly voicing its opposition. In Marseilles as well as Paris, Blanquists, Proudhonians, neo-Jacobins, and members of the Workers' International were openly critical of the declaration of war. The attitudes of radical republicans varied from region to region. In the south (Aquitaine, Languedoc, and the Pyrenees), radicals resolutely opposed the war. In Dordogne their position appears to have been similar,[7] as it was also in Vienne, to judge by the attitude of the newspaper *Le National*. In Tarn, radical republicans were even more outspoken. Early in August "old soldiers traveling by rail to join their regiments or staging areas were accosted in the vicinity of the station by leaders of the [democratic] party, who exhorted them to shoot at their leaders and at the emperor rather than at the Prussians."[8] Here and there, demonstrators threatened the emperor and the imperial prince, though it is hard to attach much significance to these threats. In Limoges there were already a few demonstrations in favor of the Republic.

News of French defeats at Wissemburg, Forbach, and Froeschwiller reached Paris on August 5 and 6. At this point the government began censoring bad news from the front.[9] The absence of information heightened anxiety. At the time, the provinces seemed quieter than Paris. Generally speaking, anxiety spread more rapidly in the cities than in the countryside. In any case the scarcity of news opened the door to rumor. A kind of spy mania erupted. In some places there was panic reminiscent of the Great Fear of 1789.

Despite the growing anxiety, the regime's adversaries were not yet ready to declare their opposition to the war. To be sure, early support for the conflict began to evaporate. Many clericals and legitimists no longer hesitated to voice open disapproval of the government's policy toward Rome, particularly since preparations for municipal elections, to be held as previously scheduled on August

6 and 7, revived local political debate. But demoralization had yet to set in. People hung on the slightest rumor of victory. Denying the obvious, they tried to exorcise the specter of defeat, to which they refused to resign themselves.

Meanwhile, however, rural areas were already suffering from the unexpected magnitude of the conflict. Service in the local national guard was reinstated for all able-bodied males between the ages of thirty and forty. The entire cohort of young men reaching the age of conscription in 1870 was called up ahead of schedule. And all veterans under thirty-five, whether married or not, were called back to active service. All of these things came as unpleasant surprises.[10] And so it was in Hautefaye,[11] although there, as in most other communes, nothing had yet been done about organizing a local guard unit.[12] In the summer of 1870, the public still had given no thought to a general mobilization. The murder of Alain de Monéys took place at a time of mass conscription conducted in a climate of anxiety but not despair.[13] Optimism about the war remained widespread, as evidenced by the large number of men who volunteered to defend French soil. The murder victim himself shared this optimism.

On August 9, the day the Ollivier ministry fell, a mob of 10,000–30,000 republicans demonstrated noisily in front of the Palais Bourbon, calling for the downfall of the emperor. There were also incidents in Toulon, Marseilles, Mâcon, Montpellier, and Le Creusot. In Limoges the crowd shouted "Vive la République!" In Angoulême on August 8 and in Périgueux on August 9, citizens gave free vent to anticlerical sentiments.[14] The seminary in the prefecture of the Dordogne was devastated.[15]

It is impossible to know what those present on the fairground of Hautefaye on August 16 knew of these various movements, which constitute what is sometimes referred to as the "pre–Fourth of September" [in allusion to the date when the empire was finally overthrown—*Trans.*]. On August 16 a fierce but indecisive battle was fought at Rezonville, and for a brief time an overly optimistic interpretation of the outcome rekindled French hopes. We do know that people at the Hautefaye fairground commented on the defeats sustained by French forces between August 4 and August 6. The climate at the fair was one of anxiety, although the terrible drought of the summer of 1870 in a sense overshadowed the bad news from the war. Peasants, aware that the emperor had joined his troops at the front, worried about his fate.[16] They feared for the regime and worried about their own future. According to the prefect, the departure of soldiers for the front had been the occasion of scenes of despair in parts of Dordogne. People began to speak of a Prussian presence in nearby regions. In short, the circumstances seemed ripe for a renewal of the Great Fear.

Anxiety did not imply readiness to give up—on the contrary. The bad news from the front led people from all over the country to seek more direct involvement.[17] Meanwhile, the peasants of Périgord and Charente found new grounds for hostility toward republicans. As early as 1869 the language of Périgueux radicals had already taken on a newly aggressive tone. Louis Mie, for example, did not shrink from branding the emperor a tyrant and an adventurer.[18] With the news of military defeat, the republican avant-garde took heart. On August 7 the radicals gained the upper hand in Nontron, according to later comments by Gambetta's young friend Alcide Dusolier. On the tenth they began openly condemning the emperor. The population in this subprefecture was now convinced that a republic was inevitable.[19] The leaders of the Bonapartists, or at any rate of the so-called *plébiscitaires,* reportedly went into hiding. If this report is accurate, then the leaders, obviously hesitant and discouraged, were a long way from sharing the defiance of their rural followers, who were prepared to defend their sovereign. Leaders and followers presumably reacted differently because they viewed the unfolding tragedy in different lights. In any case, the peasants assembled on the fairground of Hautefaye on August 16 were most likely aware of the militant antigovernment posture of the republicans in Nontron, just ten miles away. Given that their own patriotism was now at fever pitch, their irritation is understandable.

The area was rife with contradictory rumors. One consequence of the murder was to reveal the sheer diversity of what was being said. Of course, most of the reports concerned not republicans but nobles and curés. On the basis of what the Hautefaye affair revealed, it seems that both the press and the government underestimated the intensity of antiaristocratic feeling. Hatred of the nobility appears to have welled up from the remote past. Peasants believed that the Prussians, supported by French nobles, would return the king to France in their wagons, as they had done in 1815.[20] People in

Périgord believed, incorrectly, that the nobility was as unmoved as ever by patriotic feelings and in league with aristocrats from the other side of the Rhine. The Prussians would pillage and burn peasant homes, as they had done before.[21] They would rape wives and daughters. But they would carefully avoid damage to aristocratic châteaux. And rural priests were not only envied for their exemption from the draft but accused of saying prayers for the emperor's enemies.

This hostility to nobles and priests was by no means confined to Périgord. In the Somme district, the comte d'Estourmel, a notorious legitimist, was threatened in his own castle.[22] In Haut-Rhin, there were attacks on a republican member of the Corps Législatif. In Tarn and Gard, Protestants were openly accused of collusion with Prussia.[23] In Burgundy, peasants believed that priests were sending all the alms they collected to the enemy.

In Périgord, however, the rumors seem to have been more narrowly focused. Caution is in order: the investigation that followed the murder no doubt turned up rumors and protests that may have gone unnoticed elsewhere. Rumor was rife in Vienne, for example. At Châtellerault, people chased Prussian spies. In mid-August an individual wrongly suspected of intelligence with the enemy was attacked. "Down with the Prussian! Drown the Prussian!" shouted the unruly mob. The unfortunate target of this hostility turned out to be an employee of the railroad.[24] Priests in the tiny communes of Vezières and Beuxes were accused of being enemy agents. In Beuxes the priest was followed and "ashes were scattered on his path at night" to thwart his skullduggery.[25] Several days before August 16, at the fairground in Charras, a small town in the Charente, there were reports of slogans identical to those responsible for triggering the murder in Hautefaye.[26] The two villages were less than seven miles apart.

The murder investigation would reveal that threats against priests were common in the region, particularly in the Nontron district. The justice of the peace of Champagnac-de-Belair found that various residents of Cantillac had accused the venerable curé of Saint-Pancrace of sending money to the Prussians. At Sceau-Saint-Angel the same charge was leveled at the marquis Amédée de la Garde.[27] In Saint-Paul-de-Lizonne an antique dealer found himself threatened by outraged parishioners when it was felt that he had been staring too hard at the church's frescoes.[28] The emperor was being betrayed by nobles and priests who were sending money to the Prussians: rural folk were firmly convinced of this, Alcide Dusolier tells us. "Figures were cited," he wrote in 1874. "The curé of V. . . had sent 16,000 francs; the comte de G. . ., 25,000 francs; and so on."[29] Once again, precise numbers lent credence to rumors of imaginary transfers of cash.

Similar rumors stirred up trouble in the neighboring district. On the day after the murder, the imperial prosecutor in Ribérac detailed these rumors in a report to his superior: "The justice of the peace of Neuvic wrote to me [on August 13] that the peasants in his canton blame our disasters on the meeting of the bishops in Rome—the Vatican Council—and on the French clergy, which is alleged to have sent the Prussians some of Saint Peter's pence."[30] "Yesterday [August 17], the justice of the peace of Verteillac and several other individuals informed me that several priests, in particular the curés of this parish and of Nanteuil, had said things suggesting that they rejoiced in our enemies' success." The curé of Vendoire (as well as the one in Cherval) allegedly said that "he was keeping his most delicate dishes and best wine for the Prussians." After church, the curé of Lusignac supposedly challenged a group of young men who were about to leave for the front: "You're greasing your boots to go get yourselves killed! . . . Personally, I'm staying." The curé of Villetoureix, "known for his legitimist opinions, his violent character, and his ultramontane views, allegedly made a joke of the same sort to a member of the mobile guard." When some people went after him, a Ribérac magistrate intervened and dispersed the hostile crowd. The prosecutor asked the curé of the subprefecture to urge the clergy to conceal its views. "There can be no doubt," he added, "that these gentlemen were pained by the sight of our troops leaving Rome and that in expressing their regret they voice hopes that run counter to national feeling." Once again we see the logic of the Dordogne peasants' behavior, particularly given the fact that in previous years the government had not hesitated to stir up their feelings against the opposition, led by legitimist nobles and the clerical party.[31] The war merely exacerbated hostility whose roots were numerous and deep.

Republicans were also a target of rumor, though antirepublican sentiment seems to have been somewhat less violent. A mob attacked Victor Jacquaud, managing editor of the *National de la Vienne,* on the fairground at Gençay. He was accused of favoring a Prussian victory. "They threatened him, jostled him, struck him . . . A friend sheltered him in his home and saved his life. The house was besieged and attacked. He managed to escape, but he owned a nearby country house. The mob moved there en masse." It took armed force to keep the place from being sacked.[32] The sequence of events is identical to what took place at Hautefaye, and it was only by chance that we do not hear of the "cannibals of Gençay" rather than Hautefaye. The tragedy of August 16 was a sign. It revealed collective psychoses, desires, and anxieties that extended far beyond the tiny commune in which the murder occurred.

Alcide Dusolier was well aware of the degree to which the peasants were convinced of an alliance between nobles and republicans. The emperor, he said, "was not to blame for any" of the French disasters. "These innocents hear that Jules Favre and Gambetta have hidden weapons" and "they repeat the absurd accusation."[33]

The young republican found it difficult to understand why these rumors created such powerful bonds in a community no longer capable of coping with its anxieties.[34] The peasants felt an urgent need to name those responsible for their misfortune so as to give a logical interpretation of a confused situation. Social psychologists have analyzed the nature and function of rumor in wartime. Often, they find, rumors "spread the virus of hostility and hatred against subgroups loyal to the nation."[35] This explanation accounts for the attitude of the peasants of the Nontron district. Credulity, moreover, is unequally distributed in any society. People hear only what they expect to hear. The figures of menace they see are those already present in their imagination. Finally, there is an overwhelming tendency to search for traitors and persecutors outside one's own group.[36]

The government's rhetoric on the eve of the war and the rumors repeated throughout the Nontron district on August 16, 1870, were thus logically consistent with the peasants' longstanding hostility toward nobles, republicans, and priests.[37] Note, in passing, the multiple meanings attached to the word "Prussian." The term was applied not to actual foreigners but to those suspected of being enemy agents or merely accused of being enemy supporters. Only at Hautefaye, in the heat of violence, did a few of the duller members of the mob actually persuade themselves that Alain de Monéys was an authentic Prussian. It took a murder to bring about a full metamorphosis of the "Prussian" from figure of the imagination to incarnation of evil.

A National Holiday in Honor of the Emperor

The tragedy at Hautefaye coincided with two celebrations: the fair of August 14–16 and the national holiday of August 15. In this particular village, a popular celebration thus overlapped with an official holiday imposed by the authorities. The ceremonies honoring the emperor fell right in the middle of the fair. The fifteenth of August is also the Feast of the Assumption, one of those *bonnes fêtes* to which—even in regions, like the Nontron district, which were not noted for religious fervor—peasants remained attached. In Hautefaye the religious holiday was of particular importance because the titular and patron saint of the local church was Our Lady of the Assumption.[38] The Second Empire was able to coopt this occasion, this festival with deep roots in popular religion, and turn it to the benefit of the sovereign and the nation. It succeeded where Louis-Philippe had failed: the bourgeois monarch had never been able to stir up any genuine popular enthusiasm for his May 1 holiday, even though it marked the beginning of the month of Mary.[39]

According to the decree of February 16, 1852, which instituted the occasion, August 15 was a "national holiday" whose purpose was to commemorate the First Empire, honor the principles of 1789 (but not of 1793),[40] and celebrate the prince-president (and later the emperor). For the rural folk of Dordogne, however, it was above all the emperor's day, or, as rural mayors liked to say, "our emperor's day." On August 15, peasants celebrated their emancipation from patronage and the reconstitution of national unity under the aegis of Napoleon III.[41] In other words, the holiday deepened their awareness of their political identity.

August 15, 1870, does not seem to have been celebrated with a great deal of enthusiasm, which is hardly surprising. The archives, previously voluminous, have little to say about that year's festivities.[42] We hear only that the authorities gathered at the Saint-Front cathedral in Périgueux to hear a *Te deum*. Apparently only official ceremonies were held.

But a well-established social practice cannot be abruptly ended without a trace. According to numerous reports from the villages, the national holiday was celebrated with particular intensity in Dordogne during the 1860s. Political sentiments were loudly expressed and left their mark on the reveling crowds. Some mayors were in the habit of using the occasion to harangue their audience, as the mayor of Sainte-Mondane did in 1865. The fifteenth of August was also an opportunity to promote municipal consciousness in rural areas. Although the clergy participated (since the occasion was also a religious holiday), it is clear that the principal beneficiaries were the mayors.[43]

The celebration of August 15 in subprefectural towns was lavish.[44] In the morning the authorities attended Mass and heard the *Te deum*. The official delegation marched through streets decorated with flags by day and illuminated by night.[45] Meat and bread were distributed to the poor in honor of the sovereign. The popular celebration began in the afternoon. In Nontron in 1869, the hundredth anniversary of the birth of Napoleon I, the events included a greased-pole climb, a horseshoe toss, and a wheel of fortune. A modern "velocipede" race replaced the old-fashioned potato race in 1865. In the evening there was dancing, followed by fireworks. In short, the celebration of August 15 in Nontron may have drawn its inspiration from the royal festivals of the July Monarchy, but in many respects it foreshadowed the Bastille Day celebrations of the Third Republic.[46]

For our purposes we are interested in how the holiday was observed not in subprefectural towns but in small villages. Perhaps the most striking aspect of the celebration was the ringing of the bells. In some communes the bellringing began the night before.[47] In any case, the sacristan was hard at work early on the morning of the fifteenth. In Eymet in 1865, the bells began at five in the morning. The streets of the commune were swept before dawn, according to the mayor of Bussière-Badil. In almost all rural parishes the curé sang the *Te deum* after High Mass. The mayor, members of the municipal council, and possibly the firemen and members of youth organizations participated in the ceremony. Everywhere the authorities dispensed charity. In Saint-Astier a meal was served to seventy-five paupers. That night there was a banquet for the members of the municipal council. Toasts were drunk in honor of the sovereign and the imperial family. Then the public celebration began. In the countryside, firecrackers, rockets, and bonfires generally took the place of fireworks displays. Almost everywhere the holiday ended with a dance. Throughout the day one could hear shouts of "Vive l'Empereur! Vive l'Impératrice! Vive le Prince impérial!" Despite the tragic turn of events, it is likely that the residents of Hautefaye and neighboring villages uttered such cries on the eve of the murder. The shouts heard on August 16 expressed sentiments similar to those voiced on the national holiday.

Consider, for example, the festivities that took place on August 15, 1866, in the town of Vieux-Mareuil, not twelve miles from Hautefaye. "Forty-five veterans and young volunteers practiced drills to be performed at the church and in the procession." When the day arrived, this contingent led the way, preceded by a drummer. The marchers went first to the town hall, where the tricolor flag was kept. Then they fired their rifles. The mayor and municipal council marched to High Mass, after which they listened to the *Te deum.* Youths and guilds took part in vespers. That night Vieux-Mareuil was illuminated to mark the occasion. "Venetian lanterns [were] hung at intervals [in the streets]." According to the mayor, "each house put up its own lights in competition with the neighbors." At eight o'clock an honor guard fired its rifles, and there was a fireworks display for the assembled residents of the commune. Next came the national guard banquet. Meanwhile, the town distributed food to the poor. Punctuated by shouts of "Vive l'Empereur!" the day ended to the strains of "Napoleonic songs."

But Vieux-Mareuil was more than a village; it was almost a small town. The August 15 ceremonies at Hautefaye were probably more like those celebrated in Saint-Front-la-Rivière, a relatively poor commune, in 1865.[48] "At vespers," the mayor wrote, "the municipal council, preceded by the national flag, went to the church to hear the *Te deum.*" This was followed by a procession through the streets of the village. At the end of this religious ceremony, the municipal council met for a "modest banquet," open to all. This "amicable gathering" ended with toasts. By ten o'clock, the mayor reports, the commune once again slumbered "in the most total silence."

Licentiousness and Boasting on the Fairground

The Hautefaye affair belongs not to the history of a commune but to the story of a fair. Little is to be gained from knowledge of the anthropological character of the people who lived in the hamlet where the crime occurred. The kinship structure of the vicinity has nothing to teach us, nor is there much to learn from an understanding of the tensions that existed within the village community. Hautefaye was at best a modest backdrop. Certain actors in the drama came from the commune, but the plot itself was not hatched in this unremarkable environment.

The territory involved in the murder was determined by the attraction of the fair. To judge by the places of residence of the twenty-one persons indicted, the fair's influence extended over a radius of about fifteen miles. The territory in question thus amounts to something over 700 square miles.[49] This area extended beyond the boundaries of the *département*. It included several cantons of Charente and stretched as far as the border of Haute-Vienne.

The exact boundaries of this region are vague. Several competing fairs drew participants from overlapping areas. A person who went to one fair one year might go to a different fair the next year. Peasants who attended the fairs in a particular region met the same people regularly, but never in the same group. Thus, the relations that sprang up on the fairgrounds or in nearby cafés and inns for the most part involved relative strangers. This is an important clue to understanding what happened at Hautefaye. The comparative anonymity of the participants, the unlikelihood of encountering people one knew well, created conditions in which people felt free to behave with unaccustomed lack of restraint.

Fairs proliferated in Dordogne during the July Monarchy.[50] In 1821 there were some ninety-one in the Nontron district alone,[51] divided among eighteen communes and distributed throughout the calendar year in a systematic fashion that deserves further study.[52] At the time of the murder, the commune of Hautefaye was fortunate in being the site of two "accredited" fairs, on August 16 and December 22. With the support of mayors from nearby villages, the municipality applied for permission to hold ten others, so that there would be a fair on the seventeenth of every month. The government turned down this request.

The market fair that was held from August 14 to August 16, in the middle of a month in which gatherings of this type were relatively infrequent, had existed for quite some time.[53] Permission to hold the fair had been granted to Jacques Conan, the local *seigneur*, by letters patent of King Louis XIII in 1633. The choice of Assumption Day in itself shows how old the institution was. In 1834 the general council voted to create two new fair days: April 17 and October 6.[54] Thus, peasants would have gathered on the fairground at Hautefaye in all four seasons. But the following year, the government, probably with an eye to limiting travel and reducing the number of lost work days, decided to rescind the new authorizations. The commune protested. At the time, one Dordogne deputy indicated that the fairs were held anyway, despite the ban, and were "truly useful for commerce. What we are asking for is not so much the creation of a new fair as legal recognition of an existing one." In any case, by the end of the Second Empire, Hautefaye was indeed the site of four annual fairs.[55]

The communal fairground was situated in open country. There was no city or town to speak of nearby. The Hautefaye fairground fitted the anthropologists' definition: "An empty, unclaimed area that is filled at regular intervals."[56] The fair was nothing more than a periodic morning gathering of males. Here the upper strata of the peasantry, the owners of small to medium-sized plots, mingled with the stewards and tenant farmers of the leading landowners.[57] A few artisans—blacksmiths, gelders, wheelwrights—came to offer their services.[58] Livestock dealers and hawkers also showed up. In Hautefaye on August 16, 1870, not one *petit bourgeois* was in evidence after two in the afternoon, except for a notary seated at a table in the inn. Of course it was said later that some had prudently fled the scene. As we have seen, the nobles of the Nontron district did not disdain to mingle with the wealthier merchants and peasants at the fair. But generally they were accompanied by servants or tenant farmers who knew the scene.

In Nontron, the *fête du comice,* or agricultural show, was an occasion for rural society to honor its own hierarchy; carefully organized, controlled, and supervised, the show was an occasion for the government and the elite to make the point that modernization served everyone's interests.[59] By contrast, the fairground at Hautefaye was a place where peasants could hear their own voices and mingle with their own kind. There was no need for restraint or feigned humility or deference as peasants went through the rituals of the day, talked and traded, voiced opinions, jeered enemies, and puffed themselves up with boasts.

The Hautefaye fair was not really a place where country met city. What contact there was was highly mediated. From the fourteenth to the sixteenth of August, the distinction between fairground and village was eroded. The fair spilled over into a communal seat that was really no larger than a hamlet. For the space of these few days, houses and storage sheds were converted into tumultuous, improvised inns.[60] The overwhelming importance of the fair tended to push the women of Hautefaye into the shadows. Not many women, it seems, came to the fair. The handful of wives and daughters in the village were lost amid the hundreds of men gathered on the fairground. Significantly, the commune was never able to support a market.[61]

In 1870 this type of fair was an anachronism.[62] Hautefaye was not an easy place to reach. The roads were ancient, one sign that this fair was not a modern institution. Although many who attended came from Charente, no road linked Hautefaye to that *département*. Buyers and sellers reached the fairground via footpaths, said to be quite practicable.

Fairs, of course, were apt to exist in outlying areas, on regional borders, where the produce of one type of farmland could be traded for that of another. This was the case at Hautefaye. The location of the fairground, in the open country on the boundary between two *départements* and two natural regions, made this function particularly visible. It also increased the likelihood that there would be no supervisory authorities. On August 16, 1870, this factor proved crucial. No gendarme visited Hautefaye that day, and, as I mentioned earlier, no local guard unit had yet been organized in the commune. Such a total absence of law enforcement was unusual, as is evident from reports of the gendarmerie's activities in the region. In 1859, for example, Dordogne gendarmes inspected 16,572 taverns, oversaw 370 festivals, and monitored 2,724 fairs and markets.[63] Hence it is surprising that there were no gendarmes in Hautefaye on August 16, 1870. Perhaps this should be seen as an indication of the collapse of authority that some say marked the last days of the Napoleonic regime.

During the nineteenth century there was a sharp decline in the number of fairs held on open grounds in the heart of the country.[64] But peasants were fond of these traditional gatherings, which afforded an opportunity to sample pleasures that no urban fair could provide. For them, these border fairs were exciting events, occasionally spiced by violence.

The authoritarian imperial government had sought, in

Dordogne at any rate, to rationalize trade (both geographically and chronologically) and to encourage urban fairs, which were more easily monitored and more conveniently situated in relation to the new channels of commerce. The government soon began cracking down on illegal assemblies. In 1853 the administration closed some of the less important border fairs. In April the authorities, supported by big landowners, attempted to ban customary fairs at Port-Sainte-Foy, close to the border between Dordogne and Gironde. The hamlet in which these makeshift fairs were held belonged to two different communes, Saint-Avit-du-Tizac and La Roquette. The closest town, Sainte-Foy-la-Grande, already the site of fifteen fairs each year, declared its opposition to these traditional events, now seen as competition. When ordered to disperse, the peasants who had gathered on the temporary fairground at Port-Sainte-Foy "withdrew . . . but only to move off into nearby fields, where they continued their transactions."[65]

The following month, gendarmes blocked the roads and tried to close down the illegal fair. Around two in the afternoon, however, "drovers moved rather substantial herds of livestock across country into a newly plowed field, probably chosen beforehand for just this purpose."[66] The gendarmes sought warrants to arrest those responsible. According to the subprefect of Bergerac, this action constituted an alarming case of "passive resistance," all the more worrisome in that similar unauthorized gatherings were taking place in Vélines, Saint-Méard-de-Gurçon, and Le Fleix. The minister of the interior held that these gatherings were customary affairs. Since the peasants claimed to be attached to them and had shown themselves determined to resist, with force if necessary, he recommended compromise.[67] The prefect therefore chose the course of tolerance.

On the sixteenth of August, a livestock fair was held at Hautefaye. Husbandmen went to the fair not only to sell their stock but also to demonstrate their prowess. Farmers traveled alone, wearing their peasant smocks or perhaps their outfits *de petite sortie*—that is, better clothes reserved for minor occasions. In their right hands these peasants carried clubs or prods, because the fairground was a place where symbols were brandished with pride. Bargaining and animal handling were done with flair, a fact that we should bear in mind when the time comes to analyze the circumstances of the murder. The purpose of the prod was not to guide but to "touch" the animal, that is, to poke it in the flanks or tickle it under the thighs. Using his hand, the seller showed off the animal by opening its eyes and mouth.[68]

"Behind the teeming, apparently anarchic spectacle" of the fair lay a "complex order."[69] Events were carefully scheduled. Animals were shown in the morning. The peasant looked for a good spot to show any animals he hoped to sell. For hours on end he negotiated and bargained. Then came the time for *bourrades,* or insults; the period for joking came later. On the fairground, young peasants learned how to exhibit livestock and estimate an animal's value. They also learned the rituals of masculinity. The fair was an opportunity for husbandmen to demonstrate their mettle. Boasts were made and challenges laid down in the presence of a large and discerning audience. Honor and prestige were on the line.[70] It was of the utmost importance for each man to demonstrate his perspicacity and shrewdness, his discerning eye.

In the afternoon, symbolism gave way to celebration. Tired of animals, the peasant abandoned the sounds and smells of the fairground and the buzzing insects for a table in an inn. It was at this stage that the onlookers arrived. On August 16, 1870, Alain de Monéys turned up at two o'clock, fairly late in the day, allegedly to buy a heifer to be given to an indigent family. By that hour the fairground had become a permissive, not to say licentious, place.[71] It was this licentiousness that aroused the wrath of prominent citizens.[72] The tension of bargaining gave way to a time of relaxation, and, as the hours passed, some were tempted to step over the line between decency and impropriety. By evening the fairground became a place where violence was likely to erupt—more likely there than on the street, at any rate.[73]

For one thing, everybody came to drink, and we may assume that on the afternoon of August 16, 1870, the heat stimulated their thirst.[74] Hautefaye's makeshift inns and cafés served a restricted clientele. They were places not only for drinking but also for making deals. It was a time when dodges were disclosed, when an animal's hidden flaws were revealed to general laughter. What took place on the fairground was serious business; now came the time for fun. Gambling, however, was prohibited. Since 1859, games of chance and even innocent card games had been prohibited in cafés and taverns at fairgrounds by order of the prefect of Dordogne.[75] Since there were no gendarmes on the scene, however, it is difficult to know whether this edict was respected.

Once the business was wrapped up, talk went on interminably in the inns. On the afternoon of the fair the peasant lost track of time, and the slow pace of Alain de Monéys's torture reflected this carefree attitude. Fair days were a time to stop work and go chat with others who shared the same jargon and were fond of talk. They offered an opportunity to escape from the rather oppressive atmosphere of the village, where everyone knew everyone else, and a chance to exchange and comment on news of the outside world. The inn became a temple in which rumor and politics were gods. But distance from the city and from the authorities made it the antithesis of a forum.[76] On August 16, 1870, the scene in Hautefaye contrasted sharply with that in Nontron's central square, near which townfolk gathered in the Italian café.

On that day, the peasants who had assembled in Hautefaye's taverns had many things to worry about, many grounds for anxiety. Foremost among these was the drought.[77] Peasants, particularly those who grew crops for market, had been suffering its effects since 1868. By August 1870 there had been little rain for almost six months, and even livestock farmers were feeling the effects. Bitter complaints had been heard since the time of the hay harvest in June. "Fountains, wells, and lakes [had been] almost dry" for some time.[78] Never in living memory had the waters of the Isle stood at such a low level in Périgueux. By mid-August the situation was desperate. In the words of the *procureur général,* "fodder is everywhere in short supply, and the price of hay has more than doubled. Farmers are therefore finding it extremely difficult to feed and maintain their livestock, and a great deal of stock is being sold off," with a consequent drop in price.[79] Worse still, the number of animals already slaughtered had dried up demand, and it was becoming impossible for peasants to find dealers willing to take their remaining animals off their hands.

The bad news from the front was also discussed in the inns of Hautefaye. Léonard, known as Piarrouty, the *peillaro* (ragpicker) of Nontronneau, had just learned that his son, who had sold his services as a replacement conscript to an agent of the house of Pons, had been killed, probably "blown to bits." It was hardly surprising that he should want to avenge his son's death by treating the body of the "Prussian" as he had learned to treat the carcass of an animal. For two days, people in Hautefaye had heard rumors blaming the disaster on nobles, priests, and republicans and had been worrying about the fate of the emperor and his dynasty.

The crime of Hautefaye is inseparable from the events of the fair. What happened on August 16 cannot be understood without first understanding the character of the fair. The young nobleman was murdered during a licentious interlude made worse by the absence of law enforcement and a vague sense of vacuum at the center. The crime took place in the afternoon, a time of drinking, debauch, and talk which on the day of the murder was not only unbridled but also anguished. It was a time of bragging and bravado, of a weakening of village norms enforced by everyone's being known to everyone else. In this anxious climate, people felt a growing urge to celebrate and reinforce their political unity and shared emotions by participating in some spectacular collective act.

The staging of the drama was dictated by the very schedule of the fair: it was an "accumulation of rapid, overlapping actions involving many different individuals."[80] If it is true that fairs of this type were the "ideal place for [grasping] the organic relation of peasant society to the dominant surrounding society," then the murder of August 16, 1870, can be interpreted as a sign of the intensity of the conflict between the peasants of the Nontron district and all the forces that surrounded and overshadowed them.[81]

The Empty Stage

The murder was not, as the textbooks say, the work of the inhabitants of Hautefaye. It did, however, take place within the boundaries of the commune, so that it is worth taking time to describe the scene of the crime. The commune forms a tiny piece of the Nontron district, which itself seems to belong to the plateaus of lower Limousin yet which was somehow inadvertently attached to Périgord. A region of rolling hills covered with forests and meadowland, this portion of the Chestnut Belt, along with nearby Limousin,[82] was already suffering in 1870 from the dark image painted by its leading citizens, an image whose chief stereotypes were poverty, primitiveness, and lack of cultivation. This was the land of milk and chestnuts, where wheat was practically unknown and peasants still fed their hogs on acorns. The bodies of its inhabitants, according to the marquis de Mallet, were encrusted with "something like scale."[83]

The indices most commonly used by historians admittedly reinforce this negative description. Conscripts from the region were of relatively short stature and in poor health, and illiteracy was widespread in both northern Dordogne and the southern part of Haute-Vienne.[84] Soon the celebrated Professor Paul Broca and his student Collignon would make these regions the heart of the "black stain" they detected in the center of France's anthropological map.[85] Later, Edmond Demolins would offer a theory about the effects of the chestnut in hindering "the expansion of the race."[86]

The Nontron district, like Limousin, was what I have elsewhere called a "sedentary" region. Its people did not participate in the temporary migrations that proved so profitable to the inhabitants of La Marche and the mountains of Creuse and Corrèze. Marie Cappelle's sinister manor, Le Glandier, was not far from Hautefaye, nestled in a similar landscape.[87] The Lafarge affair, which excited France during the July Monarchy, unfolded in a setting similar to that of the Hautefaye murder, which left a bloody mark on the end of the Second Empire. Even today, the traveler approaching Nontron from Châlus and passing the foot of the heights on which the small town stands will sense the isolation of the place, as he makes his way along the deserted roads that wind through the chestnut groves. Only after reaching the Hautefaye promontory will he suddenly discover the vast horizons of Charente, which alleviate the strong feeling of confinement and bring a sense of contact with the outside world. Standing at the top of the slope and facing the west wind, the visitor is keenly aware of the boundary separating the two *départements*.

Another, invisible boundary also passes through Hautefaye. It is the boundary between the canton of Nontron, a district of smallholders and tenant farmers dominated by a Voltairean bourgeoisie, and the "little Vendée" of Beaussac and Mareuil, an area under the thumb of aristocratic landowners, many of them legitimists with large estates. The distribution of property within the commune reflects this duality of social structures. When the cadastral survey was taken, the Monéys family owned 166 hectares, 80 of which fell

within the commune of Hautefaye.[88] The rest of the commune
longed to a handful of peasant smallholders.

In 1870 the center of the village comprised fifteen to seven
houses sheltering forty-five residents.[89] It has not changed much
then. The fairground was moved in the late 1870s.[90] A p
garden was turned into a small public park. And quite rece
modest town hall was built. That exhausts the list of ch
Today's visitor can easily imagine the scene of the crime, al
it takes some effort to blot out the tall weeds that grow
springtime in some of the alleyways down which the unfo
Alain de Monéys attempted to flee. In other respects, not
changed. The tiny church is still hemmed in by a handful c
and the maze of footpaths remains. The center of Haut
looks like a nineteenth-century hamlet.

The farmlands worked by Hautefaye's peasants overla
those of neighboring communes. The agricultural str
particularly complex owing to the proximity of the
Charente boundary. Thus, the hamlet of Ferdinas, the
attempted fratricide in 1841,[91] belonged in the late nir
tury partly to the commune of Mainzac (in Charente)
Hautefaye (in Dordogne). Because of this overlapping,
who lived in outlying hamlets were considered "stra
central hamlet (consisting of some fifteen to sevente
these outsiders were virtually unknown. Young Vill
dent who had been born in Hautefaye, wrote the
October 9, 1870, to inform him that of the three re
mised in the affair, only one, aged either sixteen
been born in the commune. "I don't know where
nally come from. They've lived for a short time i
one of these we own five houses and in the other
the guilty party. The rest belong to the neighbori

Hautefaye's population was larger in the
than it is today. The commune boasted 388 inha
in 1851, 445 in 1861, and 409 in 1872.[93] The
just as the population was beginning to decli
marked growth earlier in the century. In twent
ber of residents had decreased 12 percent. Bu
speak of "depopulation."

A group of landowning "peasants" dominated the commune. There were no other notables in Hautefaye, hence none of the hatred fueled by rural class antagonisms. To say this, of course, is to neglect those minor fissures that run through even the most seemingly homogeneous of rural communities. But there were no great landowners, no professional men, and no government officials or civil servants other than the schoolteacher, the roadmender, and the postman. Indeed, Pierre Villard, who served as postman, declared himself to be a "farmer-landowner." The mayor, Bernard Mathieu, was the blacksmith. The members of his council were farmers or artisans practicing a number of trades. François Villard called himself a mechanic; Elie Mondout an innkeeper, tobacconist, and carpenter.[94] The income of council members, as estimated by the prefecture, ranged from 500 to 3,000 francs, with a median of 800 francs.[95] It would be a mistake, however, to assume that municipal elections in Hautefaye were uneventful affairs. During the trial, Bernard Mathieu turned red with rage at the mere mention of the fights that had erupted at the last election.[96]

Presumably the sources of conflict lay elsewhere. One would have thought that this little peasant republic would have been locked in struggle with the residents of the château de Bretanges, which owned a small part of the commune. At the trial, oddly enough, no one spoke about this, as if the generosity of the Monéys had somehow defused the hostility. If there were no notables in Hautefaye, there were also few indigents forced to beg in order to stay alive. According to the curés of the parish, the number of beggars never exceeded seven or eight at any time during the Second Empire.[97]

The state of education was deplorable, but no worse than elsewhere in the region. In 1837 half of the municipal councillors could write their names. Of the nine citizens who paid the most taxes, only two were capable of this feat.[98] The first primary school opened its doors in 1847, fourteen years after passage of the Guizot Law.[99] In 1852, when the population of the commune was 468, only nine boys (even in the summer) attended this school, whose master was quite mediocre.[100] In 1869, out of a population of 445, twenty boys and fifteen girls attended school; ten boys and thirteen girls of school age received no schooling whatsoever. Yet the situation was actually better than in the rest of the canton, where a total of 957 children were in school while 1,178 remained outside.[101] The consequences

are clear. Of 152 youths in the cohort of 1869 called upon to draw lots in the canton of Nontron, 55, or only 36 percent, said they knew how to read and write.[102]

Bad as things were, considerable progress had been made in education under the Second Empire. As we saw earlier, the commune of Hautefaye had already produced one law student, the son of a family regularly represented on the municipal council. Yet in 1892, when a bishop asked the curé of Hautefaye what his parishioners read, the curé replied: "In Hautefaye no one reads."[103]

Despite the low level of religious practice, it was the fervent wish of commune residents that their curé live among them. In 1848 the municipal council resorted to a modest form of blackmail: the produce of the presbytery garden and clover from the church grounds would be withheld from the priest so long as he refused to reside in Hautefaye. In 1866 the council decided to repair the presbytery and church in the hope that the authorities would appoint a resident curé, and an appointment was made the following year.[104] At the time of the murder, then, the "curé"[105] had been in residence for only three years, too short a period for possible resentments to have turned rancid.

The minutes of the municipal council reflect conscientious efforts at improvement.[106] The council worried constantly about the roads. In 1870 it asked for construction of a road link with the Charente. In 1847 it approved the hiring of a schoolteacher. In 1850 it called for daily mail deliveries. The building of a new cemetery was the big project for the early years of the Empire. Foul odors had been detected emanating from the old cemetery in the center of town. The new one, located far from any dwellings, was to be surrounded by walls. Finally, in 1868, the council approved the creation of a new charity bureau. Yet Hautefaye had no town hall. The council met at the home of Bernard Mathieu, the blacksmith. After he was forced out of office, the meetings moved to the schoolteacher's home. A fact more important for our purposes is that in 1870 the commune had still not been assigned a rural policeman. In truth, the issue that most interested the councillors of Hautefaye—at one time their pride and joy but soon to become a source of shame—was the organization of the fairs and the license fee that was collected each time one was held.

We know the political sentiments of the residents of Hautefaye.

In December 1851, all who voted expressed approval of the coup d'état. The vote was again unanimous in the plebiscite of 1852. On May 8, 1870, the 117 voters in the commune voted "yes," and only eleven voters abstained. The emperor thus received the votes of 92 percent of those registered.[107]

For nearly a century Hautefaye would remain a symbol of savagery, yet court records reveal no unusual propensity to violence. In 1841 there was an attempted fratricide in one of the commune's hamlets. In 1864 the cantonal commissioner reported a burglary that resulted in the theft of 750 francs.[108] In November 1870 a young girl was raped.[109] But sexual violence was commonplace in rural areas during the Third Republic.[110]

Given the pettiness of Hautefaye's preoccupations, the reader will already have concluded that the horrible crime committed there can hardly be blamed on the nature of the place. The significance of the crime does not lie in its setting. Local history can, however, enlighten us about certain necessary conditions: the delay in organizing the national guard, the absence of a rural policeman, the lack of any prominent local citizens with enough authority to calm the crowd and of educated people prepared to urge greater humanity. Against the outburst of peasant violence, Hautefaye could erect no other dike than the authority of its mayor, and that authority was sorely lacking.

This unusual absence of authority left the field clear for the customary hate-filled shouts to escalate into murderous acts. What was unusual about the event was not the way it started but the fact that it was allowed to run its course. The absence of all authority permitted the unimpeded execution of a lethal plan that the peasants of the Nontron district had long proclaimed to be their wish but had always been prevented from carrying out.[111]

With the stage now set, the props in place, and the prologue complete, the victim draws near. It is two in the afternoon, August 16, 1870. The fair is in full swing.

3

The Celebration of Murder

The Designation of the Victim

Alain de Monéys had managed his family's estates for some years. It was in this role that he went to the fairground on August 16. He lived in the château de Bretanges, situated on high ground midway between the hamlets of Hautefaye and Beaussac. Short and prematurely bald, Monéys was still unmarried at the age of thirty-two. Army medical examiners had exempted him from service on grounds of a "weak constitution." He enjoyed a local reputation for politeness and generosity. Of course, the tragic circumstances surrounding his death inevitably caused people to describe him in glowing terms.

His father, Amédée descended from a line that included a number of naval officers, reportedly took a passionate interest in oceanography and the literature of exploration.[1] Interested in agronomy as well, he had had part of his land cleared for vineyards. His son Alain looked forward to modernizing the estate. He had just completed plans for a drainage system and hoped some day to farm the Nizonne basin.

Amédée de Monéys served as mayor of Beaussac from 1848 to 1853. Apparently he gave up the post because he was tired of serving. His son joined the municipal council in 1865 and was named first *adjoint* of the commune.[2] The Monéys were not outspoken about their political beliefs, unlike their cousin Camille de Maillard, who at twenty-six was the self-appointed leader of Little Vendée's legitimists. Although the family's discretion makes it difficult to say for sure, it seems likely that, while the Monéys of Ordières paid lip service to the emperor, that was the extent of their support. Three times a year they allegedly hosted a meeting at Bretanges of a small group of Périgord legitimists led by the new baron de Damas, who lived in the château de Hautefort.[3] There are, however, no documentary grounds for doubting the sincerity of Alain de Monéys, who for two hours insisted on his devotion to the emperor and the imperial dynasty.[4] In any case, shortly before he was murdered, he had taken steps to have his exemption from military service rescinded and had even made up his mind to enlist—striking evidence of the ephemeral climate of national unity that marked the beginning of the war.

According to the tenant farmer François Mazière, known as Sillou,[5] Camille de Maillard had made certain provocative statements on the town square in Charras on August 9, the day of a fair. "The emperor is done for," Maillard is alleged to have announced in a peremptory tone after reading his newspaper. "He's out of ammunition *(cartouches)*."[6] This lucid but pessimistic analysis of the military situation aroused indignation. "If there had been any number of us that day," Mazière told his landlord on the night of August 16, "we would have taken care of him then. But there were only four or five. Today there were more than eighty . . . Our only regret is that we let the other one [i.e., Maillard] get out alive."[7] This testimony is interesting, because it suggests that the murder may have been premeditated—its victim, Monéys, substituted only when the intended victim, Maillard, slipped through the murderers' hands.

When asked about the earlier incident while standing with several tenant farmers on the fairground at Hautefaye, Maillard, as quick to perceive the danger to himself as he had been to grasp the plight of the emperor, beat a hasty retreat. Wearing light boots, he easily outran peasants slowed by heavy wooden shoes. The plan to murder Maillard having collapsed, the mob's enmity now focused on another: it was at that moment that Alain de Monéys arrived on the scene. Approaching the village, he unwittingly provoked anger by refusing to admit that his cousin could have shouted "Vive la République!"

This transfer of hostility was facilitated by the fact that the peasants assembled on the fairground knew little about who the communal authorities were and even less about other local notables. It seems unlikely that the crime was premeditated. During the trial, Bernard Mathieu, the mayor of Hautefaye, told of one rioter's threats against him: "'We know who you are because of your belt,'" he said, pointing to my sash [symbol of the mayoral office]. 'Get lost or we'll do the same to you.'" This testimony suggests that the mob knew local officials not by sight but only by recognizable marks of office.

Chambort, a blacksmith from the Charente hamlet of Pouvrière who quickly emerged as the leader of the murderous mob, knew neither his fellow accused nor the victim, or so his attorney claimed during the trial. The murderers, according to the uncontradicted statements of their counsel, "did not know one another. Nor did they know the unfortunate Monsieur de Monéys. It was only by chance that they came together and became murderers." None of this should come as a surprise, given what we know about the circumstances surrounding the Hautefaye fair.

The refusal to acknowledge the victim's true identity is, at first sight, more surprising. Several of Monéys's friends vouched for him throughout his torture. The mob refused to listen. Most of them thought they were attacking not a noble, a great landowner, but a "Prussian" who had shouted "Vive la République!"

What we ordinarily think of as characteristic features of life in a small village, familiarity and solidarity, played no role in the Hautefaye crime. Alain de Monéys was a local, a man with property in the vicinity. His family owned eighty hectares within the boundaries of Hautefaye itself. He lived scarcely two miles away. Yet the peasants on the fairground refused, if not to consider him one of their own, at least to identify him as such when his life was on the line. Of course the conflicts and tensions inherent in rural society are sometimes a source of enmity, but such emotions did not play a part in this crime, at least not explicitly. The confrontation was not about local matters.

Chambort, the mob's ringleader, recognized that the people in Hautefaye on the day of the crime were strangers to one another and not bound by local allegiances. Sensing a vacuum, he plunged in and shamelessly usurped the role of municipal officials, who had chosen discretion over valor. Listen to the indictment: "Georges Mathieu [one of Monéys's defenders] said to [Chambort], in vain: 'But listen, you poor fool, he's your neighbor.' 'He's no more my neighbor than [he is] anyone else's . . . He's an enemy, who must be made to suffer and die' . . . He [Chambort] passed himself off as a member of the municipal council of Hautefaye or Beaussac, and he put on such an air of authority that people believed, as he himself admits, that he was the *adjoint* of Hautefaye."

In fact, as we shall soon see, the murder was by no means a settling of local scores. Nevertheless, the same insistence on unanimity that we encountered in the affair of the 45 centimes can be found here. In 1928 Judge Simonet did historical research on the case and even questioned survivors. One person wrote that "the way those lunatics saw it, everyone had to have a hand in torturing the victim. One person struck the man, then stood aside so that somebody else could have a turn, and so on until they'd all had a shot."[8] Pascal Tamisier, one of the victim's defenders, estimated that more than two hundred people had physically attacked Alain de Monéys. Onlookers were taunted, just as they had been in 1848. On the day after the murder, Jean Peltout heard Manem, who was not among those accused of the crime, say that "anybody who tries to help Monsieur de Monéys will have to deal with me. Gentleman or peasant [note the representation of society], one of us will be left beaten to a pulp."

By successfully fleeing the scene, Camille de Maillard had thrown down a challenge of his own to the peasants at the fair, a challenge that had yet to be picked up. The mob therefore forgot about the man who had started the whole thing and circulated the rumor that Alain de Monéys himself had shouted "Vive la République!" They set out to prove that this time they had caught a genuine "Prussian." The victim was not accused of shouting "Vive Henri V!" which would have been logical but superfluous. The slogan "Vive la République!" was more effective in bringing together everything the peasants hated into one focal point of violence. It established what might be called the "victim's equation," the formula that revealed his true identity:

Alain de Monéys = noble + republican = "Prussian."

At this point the first blows were struck. The curé quickly and courageously intervened. Revolver in hand, he jumped his garden wall and attempted to free the unfortunate young man. Along with the few good souls who came to his aid, he quickly grasped the logic of the crime and the significance of the victimization equation. In fact, several voices in the crowd proposed going after the curé as well. Anna Juge (Madame Antony) arrived at two-thirty and heard

Dupin say, possibly a little later: "We've killed that one [not yet true], now let's go after the curé. We'll burn the scoundrels and lay them out in a cross." The crowd applauded. When the victim's body was burned some time later, young Antonin Antony heard the peasants shout, "We must make a cross with the curé and Monsieur de Monéys and then burn the two of them."[9]

The priest therefore hid in his presbytery. Monsieur Saint-Pasteur was still a young man.[10] Born in the diocese of Tarbes, ordained in Périgueux in 1864, he had served as vicar of Payzac and curé of Savignac-Lédrier before moving to Hautefaye on May 15, 1867. Thus, as he would soon have occasion to demonstrate, he knew the Périgord peasants quite well.

Alain de Monéys thus embarked on a calvary that would continue for the next two hours. With the aid of a map drawn by the borough surveyor after the crime, we can follow with great precision the progress of the cortège that accompanied the victim to his tragic end and that prodded him from station to station.[11] The torture was slow and sporadic. At each stop, the victim must have felt renewed hope. It is as if the assailants deliberately paused to allow his defenders time to act, thereby fostering hopes whose subsequent crushing further enhanced their pleasure.

The composition of the bloody procession changed constantly. Each time the victim halted, so did his murderers. Some wandered off toward the presbytery to take advantage of the free distribution of bottled wine. Others headed for the inn to boast of their exploits. Still others returned, perhaps, to their commercial bargaining. Even the principal actors occasionally left center stage to join one of the sideshows.

Hence, not all the assailants had a very clear idea of what took place. Some were aware of only parts of the action. Many seem to have followed the drama for a while, only to quit at some point along the way. Witnesses reported seeing certain individuals pass by with bloody implements. Laurent Pougny, a twenty-year-old coalman, saw Pierre Buisson in the middle of town with a stake in his hand and at the inn saw Léonard Piarrouty with a bloody hook. All the while the murder was being committed, the fair continued. The tragedy, which lasted two hours, never occupied the entirety of the crowd.

Some heard no more than distant echoes of the crime. There

were those who followed the whole thing from the comfort of their café tables. "The inns were packed with people" that afternoon, according to Brochon, the chief judge. Those most deeply involved in the murder were therefore aware that they were performing for the benefit of a large audience.

The testimony of Jean Feytou can help us understand how those who watched pieced together the action from bits and pieces of information. The young man actually witnessed the crime only at brief intervals. He watched as the mob struck the first blows. A while later he saw Léonard Piarrouty beat the victim about the head with his horrible hook. He ran to the presbytery and asked others for details of episodes he had missed. At some point he decided to go see for himself. Obviously it was a tactic of his legal defense to claim that he had been only a spectator, but many people seem indeed to have participated in the crime chiefly as onlookers, a fact that did not fail to arouse the ire of Judge Brochon.

The most important of the peripheral actions took place in front of the presbytery, whose courtyard quickly filled with people. According to the indictment, some fifty individuals gathered there at around three o'clock, or roughly midway through the torture, after Chambort left the victim and went to the presbytery to act as "spokesman" for the assailants. For the curé it was a dangerous moment. Madame Antony saw Pierre Buisson, also known as Arnaud and Lirou, "grab the pointed end of his stake," which was covered with blood, and heard him say, "Look, now the sly dog is giving out drinks. My first blow will lay him low."

The curé Saint-Pasteur shrewdly avoided the trap. Unlike the victim, who would eventually offer his torturers a hogshead of wine, the priest had bottles of wine brought up from his cellar and distributed glasses to the people in the courtyard. He uncorked the bottles and personally served those who held out their glasses, even little Pierre Brut, known as Pierrette, who came "looking for him, saying 'I want to drink.'" Hence the mob never laid hands on the wine. There was no passing around of flagons or drinking from bottles. Instead, the men drank toasts with the curé, who hoped that this ritual of cordiality might break the ominous mood.[12] "The men all held their clubs high, but there was no violence." Father Saint-Pasteur honored his guests. He treated as gentlemen peasants unused to drinking bottled wine and to being treated with deference. At the crowd's insistence, the curé drank toasts to the emperor. He even went the crowd one better by insisting that the revelers also shout "Vive l'Impératrice!" and "Vive le Prince impérial!" He laid it on thick, in other words.[13] The toasts proved more effective in disarming the crowd than the desperate salutes to the emperor shouted by the hapless victim at the head of the bloody procession. Throughout the two hours of torture Alain de Monéys was in fact shouting "Vive l'Empereur!" in the hope of calming the anger of those who were slowly killing him.

Other sideshows took place in the cafés and inns, the gathering places of those who chose to stand aside and let things run their course. The victim's few defenders were unable to rouse this substantial contingent of bystanders to come to the young nobleman's defense. In one inn a notary armed with a rifle refused to join the assailants, but when he proposed to his fellow drinkers that they band together to prevent a murder, no one stood up.

The Calculus of Suffering

The torment of Alain de Monéys unfolded by stages in the center of the hamlet. In the first act the victim was taken from the field where he first heard that Camille de Maillard allegedly had shouted "Vive la République!" to the foot of a cherry tree, from which the mob briefly proposed to hang him. Along the way he was struck a number of times. The assault was initiated by the fearsome Campot brothers, aged twenty and twenty-two and already known for their brutality. The mob initially took the "spy" to the mayor's house with the intention of turning him over to the authorities. But the mayor's inadequate response failed to satisfy the assailants, and this "reasonable" plan was quickly discarded. The procession then "passed the mayor's house" on its way to the cherry tree. Thus, the plan to hang Monéys came about only after the municipal authorities failed to control the situation. Having forfeited control at the beginning, the mayor was unable to assert his authority later on.

It was during this initial act of the drama that the curé made his futile rescue attempt. Meanwhile, the hawker Brethenoux, who regretted having been the instigator of the crime, Philippe Dubois, an honest Hautefaye sawyer, and Georges Mathieu, an artisan from Beaussac, ignored the attackers' threats and courageously attempted to protect Monéys from his assailants. These defenders were joined, a short while later, by Pascal, a servant sent down from Bretanges at the first word of the assault. The defenders themselves were the target of a number of blows as they repeatedly sought to persuade the angry peasants that their victim was not a "Prussian" but a decent young fellow, in fact a neighbor whose generosity was known to some in the crowd.

The plan to hang Monéys seems to have given way after a few minutes to the idea of bludgeoning him to death. It is hard to make out any reason for the change, other than, perhaps, the volatile mood of the high-spirited mob.

The second act of the crime took place in the narrow alley between the mayor's home and blacksmith shop and his sheepfold. Each of these modest structures would become a station in the calvary of Alain de Monéys. The victim's defenders managed to help him toward the home of Bernard Mathieu. The beaten man had actually climbed one or two steps of the short stairway leading up to the door when the door was slammed shut. The mayor stammered a few soothing words but forbade the "accused" to enter his home. Buisson and François Mazière roughly dragged the young noble from the steps. There was no longer any question that the municipal authorities had chosen to stay out of whatever was about to happen. Chambort, twirling his leaded cane, brazenly assumed leadership of the mob. He ordered that the "Prussian," before being put to death, should be made to suffer. Some in the crowd proposed burning the prisoner, while others continued to call for hanging. The men holding Monéys decided to tie him to the blacksmith's bench. Meanwhile the physical assault continued. Brouillet, also known as Déjeunat, administered a savage beating. François Léonard, known as Piarrouty, the ragpicker of Nontronneau, sought to avenge his son by striking Monéys from behind with a hook used for weighing merchandise. The victim crumpled. For a moment the crowd thought that the *peillaro* had killed him.

We do not know for sure what happened inside the mayor-blacksmith's shop. When questioned in 1936, Mademoiselle Mazière, known as Zilliou, the daughter of the servant Pascal who was one of Monéys's defenders, told Gabriel Palus that the prisoner had been tied to the workbench.[14] Surviving reports of witness interrogations shed little light on this point. In any case, the mayor, who had refused to allow Monéys into his home, now suggested that the "Prussian" be locked up in his sheepfold, and this advice was followed.

For some minutes the torture stopped. Alain de Monéys enjoyed a few moments of respite, if not of hope. "He collapsed," the indictment reads, "upon reaching the far end of the barn, gasping for breath. Yet he believed he was safe. He asked that a hogshead of wine be purchased and given to his pursuers." He was willing to eat figs offered by his friends.

Soon, however, the mob's ominous grumbling began again. Chambort, the leader, talked of setting fire to the barn or ripping off the roof in order to grab the "Prussian." While the miller Boutandon courageously defended the door, Philippe Dubois advised Monéys to take off his jacket and shirt and don a peasant blouse in the hope that this might facilitate an eventual escape. But the assailants moved too quickly. The unfortunate young man, who had just begun to undress, had to dress again hastily. As the mob was about to lay hold of him once more, his defender Dubois tried a desperate maneuver to forestall the inevitable: "'Wouldn't you rather be shot than clubbed to death?' I asked him. 'Yes, yes!' he whispered. 'Let them shoot me.' 'You heard him, my friends,' I shouted to the mob, 'go get your rifles . . . No one paid any attention.'" The mob, having decided to make the "Prussian" suffer, had made up its mind to dispose of its victim in accordance with the traditional forms of massacre.

At this point Chambort, along with Buisson and some fifty others, went off to "speak their piece" at the presbytery.[15] The hostility of the mob might easily have been transferred to the curé, Father Saint-Pasteur. But the bulk of the murderous mob stood by its bloody prey, already reportedly engulfed by a swarm of flies.

The third act of the drama took place on the path between the sheepfold and the fairground. Somewhere along the way the assailants made a final decision to burn the "Prussian." Having snatched their victim from the vacillating authority of the mayor, there was no one to stop them. Clearly their intention was to reduce the "criminal" to the status of an animal: the ritual of slaughter proceeded from blacksmith's bench to sheepfold to fairground marketplace. According to the indictment, "they dragged the poor young man, whose head, according to witnesses, was like a bloody ball." The cruel Léonard (Piarrouty) struck additional blows with his terrible hook. "My friends, I am lost," Alain de Monéys is reported to have said to the few loyal souls who continued to defend him.

The defenders clung to one final hope: to get the victim to an inn along the way. But when Monéys managed to thrust his foot into the open door of one, the innkeeper, who wanted no part of what was going on, slammed the door shut. Philippe Dubois then slipped around the back and pleaded with the man to open the door, which had broken Monéys's ankle. The innkeeper replied: "They'll smash everything to pieces." At this point Monéys collapsed, "his head one black mass." Everyone thought that this time he was really dead when, to the astonishment of all, he suddenly picked himself up. In the presence of the mayor, who continued to follow the procession, the desperate "Prussian" made one last attempt to defend himself. Grabbing a stake left lying in a barn, he faced his attackers. Young Campot easily wrested the weapon from the dying man and struck him with it. Monéys then sought one last hiding place, under a wagon. He was pulled out, relieved "of another stake" with which he continued to try to defend himself, and dealt another blow, "said to be the death blow." Huge bloodstains on the ground bore witness to the ferocity of the final attack.

At this point the fourth act of the drama began. The mob vented its fury on a man who in all likelihood had lapsed into a coma. The body, according to one witness, was "trampled" and "threshed" as if it were so much wheat. Then began a somewhat truncated version of an age-old ritual: desecration of the corpse. After attempting to quarter the cadaver, François Mazière and the younger Campot each took one arm and dragged the body along the rocky trail, sometimes on its back, sometimes with the face to the ground. The "bouncing head" left blood on the rocks. "From time to time," the indictment reads, "Campot and Mazière abruptly dropped the body, and blows, which rained continuously, struck the head and legs with a wooden sound. The mayor, wearing his sash, continued to follow along." In short, the body was treated as if it had been carrion.[16] Finally, it was "violently hurled onto the stony, sloping bank of an almost dry pond."

"Pummeling" the "Prussian"

According to witnesses, the victim's body was still twitching. Let us pause at this point to take a closer look at what the participants in the drama had to say. Investigators named twenty-one individuals as having played leading roles in the crime. All twenty-one had enjoyed good reputations prior to August 16. For Judge Brochon, what made this crime so extraordinary was that such ordinary men could have committed such a savage act. It was most definitely not a common criminal offense. That is why one of the attorneys, the republican Louis Mie, attempted to save his clients by insisting that it was in fact a political act.

Not a single one of the accused was a woman, which is hardly surprising given the composition of the crowd on the Hautefaye fairground that day. Yet in this respect the mob violence at Hautefaye differs from previous and subsequent instances of mob violence. At Buzançais in 1847,[17] at Clamecy in 1851,[18] and on rue Haxo in Paris in May 1871,[19] women took an active part in the respective killings of young Chambert, the gendarme Bidan, and the prisoners of La Roquette. The murderous mob in Hautefaye does not conform to historians' idea of the revolutionary crowd. People of all ages were present. Still, the attack was led by mature men, aided by adolescents and older men. Of the twenty-one accused, twelve were thirty-one or older and three were eighteen or younger, hence only six were between the ages of eighteen and thirty. Two of the most vicious attackers were already old; five were past fifty. "Among the most zealous," the indictment reads, "the mayor pointed to an old man, the accused Sallat senior (aged sixty-two), who struck [Alain de Monéys] with his club." When Mathieu attempted to stop him, Sallat pushed him away, saying, "Listen, Mr. Mayor, this man is a scoundrel. He must be killed." And he continued to bludgeon the victim.

The participation of three young boys might seem surprising if we did not know of the traditional cruelty of children.[20] For adolescents allowed to attend the fair, the crime offered a welcome opportunity to demonstrate virility and assist the older men. The honor of lighting the bonfires of Saint John (midsummer's night) belonged to the youngest males in attendance. That holiday was still fresh in mind on the afternoon of August 16. Young Brut, who looked fourteen although he was actually sixteen or eighteen, lived in Hautefaye. Such a rare event as a gang murder right in the heart of his own commune seems to have excited him. He ran through the hamlet brandishing his bloody club and boasting of his cruelty. He even challenged another young man by the name of Feytou: "And what did you do? Did you hit him? You have no balls. You'd rather have your throat slit, like a capon." Even more terrifying was Brut's companion, Thibaud Limay, known as Thibassou, "who was not yet fourteen [and who] took cruel pleasure in beating the lifeless and bloody corpse with a large stick."

The fact that so few men between the ages of eighteen and thirty participated in the crime, though it is at odds with the usual pattern of village violence, is nevertheless easy to explain. Some of the men in this age group had gone off to war. Others were on the verge of being mobilized either as veterans or as conscripts for 1870. Still others knew that they were about to be drafted into the mobile guard unit soon to be organized in the area. Very likely, they were in no mood to go strutting about the fairground at Hautefaye. Then, too, selling animals was a job for the head of the family or the farm steward.

The geographic distribution of the residences of the accused coincided with the area from which the fair drew its clientele, a radius of roughly fifteen miles. The occupational distribution is likewise unsurprising. Of the twenty-one accused, twelve were farmers, seven artisans (a blacksmith, an ironsmith, a stonecutter, a mason, a tailor, a ragpicker, and a pit sawyer), and two laborers (a ditchdigger and a miner). The man who, armed with a leaded cane, acted as leader of the mob and shouted "'Go! Go!' with a commanding air," was, like Hautefaye's ineffective mayor Mathieu, a blacksmith.

Among the defenders of the two young nobles were a domestic, the loyal Pascal, and a tenant farmer, Corgniac, also known as Frisat. The latter apparently abetted Camille de Maillard's escape. Loyalty, moreover, seems to have been a tradition in the Corgniac family: during the Revolution, Frisat's father allegedly saved his masters by hiding them in a cave.[21] Not all tenant farmers were made of the same stuff, however: the dreadful François Mazière, Madame Antony's tenant, was one of the most violent. Note, too, that

Philippe Dubois, the most effective of Alain de Monéys's defenders, was a pit sawyer, who had nothing directly to gain from his generosity. He seems to have acted as he did out of a sentiment of humanity or perhaps, since he was a resident of Hautefaye, out of neighborly solidarity. Georges Mathieu, the mayor's nephew, was a baker and innkeeper in Beaussac who came to the defense of his commune's *adjoint*. As for the miller Boutandon, it may be that, like many members of his profession, he did not feel totally integrated into the community.

Everyone agreed after the fact that Bernard Mathieu's attitude had been deplorable. Bear in mind, however, that since 1815 many harried mayors in the region had proven totally powerless to stem outbreaks of peasant violence.[22] Mathieu was sixty-eight years old. He was apparently a kindly grandfather, whose granddaughter, aged nine, found the sight of the torture too much to bear. Obviously the man had little personal presence, and he was not the most highly regarded of the municipal council members. In the municipal elections of 1865, he received only 86 votes, and his *adjoint*, Pierre Jardry, 84, whereas Pierre Nadaud, a landlord, had received 103.[23] Mathieu probably owed his mayoral sash to his age, to the location of his house, and to his tidy fortune (on which he earned an income estimated by the prefecture at two thousand francs).

There is no doubt that the mayor did for some time try to calm the rioters. In front of the inn, a witness reported, Mathieu had shouted: "Boys, boys, calm down. If Monsieur de Monéys is guilty, he'll be taken to Mareuil." Although he closed the door of his home to the victim "for fear that they would smash his dishes," he did open his sheepfold in the hope of dispersing the mob.[24] At this point, some witnesses heard him say: "Take Monsieur de Monéys away from the front of the inn. He's blocking traffic." But Mathieu, at the trial, categorically denied having made this statement.

If there was to be violence, the mayor preferred that it take place on the fairground rather than in the center of the hamlet, indeed along the alley on which stood his house, sheepfold, and shop. Yet Mathieu witnessed what happened right up to the end, at times attempting to moderate the passions of those he knew best.

In front of the inn the mayor allegedly made certain scandalous statements, perhaps in jest. His remarks, widely reported, lent credence to the rumors of cannibalism. According to Jean Maurel, a seventy-eight-year-old roofer who lived in La Chapelle-Saint-Robert, the most zealous of the murderers allegedly told the mayor, at a point when the victim had "stopped in front of the inn," that "we want to kill him, burn him, and eat him." The mayor allegedly replied, "Eat him if you like." Word of this frightening injunction seems to have spread rapidly. Madame Antony had reported the same statement at the trial prior to Maurel's testimony. But the allegation seems to have had little foundation. When Mathieu strenuously denied having made the statement, the roofer retracted his testimony.

Once the mob realized that the authorities would not intervene, its threats grew more ominous: "There is no more law," shouted the murderers, gathered around the victim's pyre. "Now you can kill a noble as you would kill a fly or a chicken." Two slogans were repeatedly proclaimed throughout the long torture: "Vive l'Empereur!" and (referring to the victim) "He's a Prussian!" The allegation that Monéys, a nobleman, had cried "Vive la République!" remained to the end the justification for his murder. "That night," Antonin Antony testified, "François Mazière said, 'I hit him. We killed him. I'm not sorry. We'll kill many more. We killed him because he shouted "Vive la République!"'"

An analysis of the participants' rhetoric reveals three levels of representation. A small group clearly grasped the reality of the situation and was aghast at the crowd's blindness; this group consisted of those who knew Alain de Monéys perfectly well by sight and reputation. A second group consisted of those who regarded the victim as one of those nobles believed to be sending money to the enemy and hoping for a republican triumph. A third group consisted of those who, knowing nothing of the commune of Hautefaye, mistook Alain de Monéys for one of those "Prussians of the interior" persistently rumored to be roaming about the region. When the senior Etienne Campot was questioned about the reasons for his cruelty, he answered "half in patois, half in French": "People said he was a Prussian. I had never seen one." So he had grabbed him by the collar "to examine him." Antonin Antony testified that "Renaud strutted about the fire, saying, 'Don't we have enough Prussians on the border without having to worry about more in the heart of the country? This one's dead, and I for one think we've done our duty.'" From time to time he doffed his hat, raised his other hand, and shouted, "Vive l'Empereur! Vive la France!"[25]

"He must be killed! He must be made to die!" The peasants' actions were dictated by the logic of their thinking. But a decision still had to be made about the manner of putting the victim to death. It was not long coming: "He must be burned." Shortly after the torture began, frenzied assailants dragged Alain de Monéys about while proclaiming, "He shouted 'Vive la Prusse! Vive la République!'" Defendant Beauvais was continually screaming, "He must be killed! He must be burned!" The crowd that had gathered in front of the mayor's sheepfold continued to call for the victim's death. "Roast him!" they shouted, again reflecting the influence of the animal metaphor that underlay so much of the mob's action and rhetoric.[26] The crowd was simply applying the law of retaliation before the fact: "The victim had stopped moving. Someone shouted that he must be burned because the Prussians would be coming to burn us." Perhaps the initial plan of hanging was given up so quickly because the assailants unconsciously believed that a propitiatory burning of their victim might quell their own anxieties about death by fire.

Cannibalism was probably never seriously proposed, although it may have been considered for a fleeting moment. I shall come back to this point. But there were serious calls for the murder of the curés of Hautefaye and two nearby parishes, Mainzac (Charente)[27] and Lussas.

The treatment of Alain de Monéys's body—the nature of the assault and the forms of torture used—is also revealing. The mob intended not just to kill its victim but to inflict pain. "He must be made to suffer," Chambort declared repeatedly in the alley. The guillotine and firing squad were dismissed in favor of an older form of punishment—yet another sign of the inertia of representations.

"Pummel him": the mob's first act was to beat its victim, as in a brawl.[28] Blows were struck not only with fists but also with feet, and care was taken to make sure that "they strike home." After the victim was down, feet shod with wooden shoes were aimed at his kidneys, stomach, and face. Clubs were preferred to naked fists. Alain de Monéys was threshed as if he had been so much wheat, particularly during the final episode, when blows rained on his lifeless body for ten minutes, time enough for everyone to get into the act. Men armed with prods poked at his lower abdomen as they might tickle an animal on the market block. One of the killers used a wooden stick, "a pointed slat ripped from a shutter." And later, as we have seen, young Campot struck the victim with a stake he wrested from his hands.

Blades were not used, however. None of the assailants spoke of "bleeding" the "Prussian."[29] Knives, axes, clippers, or scythes were not mentioned, although a pitchfork was used at one point.[30] Bludgeoning, reminiscent of the stunning of an animal prior to slaughter, was the preferred method of attack. To prolong the torture and allow everyone to get in his licks, blows were carefully meted out. Léonard Piarrouty apparently violated some unspoken rule by striking the victim with his awful hook, which seems to have drawn some criticism. Yet people said they understood his behavior, because he had learned only two days before that his son was "in a thousand pieces."

The mob may have tortured its victim according to plan, but it did so in an undisciplined manner. The killers did not line both sides of the road, as in the September Massacres of Paris prisoners in 1792. But the Hautefaye crime was not exactly a lynching, either, nor was the mob totally wild.[31] There was implicit calculation in the crowd's behavior. The execution took precisely two hours. In fact, another reason for giving up the planned hanging so quickly was probably the need to prolong the punishment. The slow pace of the action, one of many signs of cruelty, also served to dilute responsibility.

The collective decision not to shoot the victim is hardly surprising. To have proceeded in that way would have been to pervert the meaning of the event. Such a modern form of execution, employing the very same means by which the military maintained order, would scarcely have satisfied the peasants assembled on the fairground at Hautefaye. The killers collectively wanted their victim, the epitome of all they felt threatening, to suffer while they enjoyed the spectacle.

The range of the crowd's actions nevertheless reveals the inroads made by modernity. In its own way, the Hautefaye mob shared the humanitarian sentiments that had been on the rise in Europe since the beginning of the eighteenth century. It did not indulge in the "ceremonious mutilations" that had still delighted revolutionary crowds from July 1789 to September 1792 as they had earlier delighted the "Jacques," or rebellious peasants, of southwestern France.[32] Dismembering one's enemies had become, since the Revolution, a mere figure of speech. Organs were no longer plucked from bodies. Alain de Monéys's head was not chopped off and paraded through the hamlet in public mockery. Of the old ritual all that remained was the attempt to cut up and desecrate the corpse, which was dragged like dead meat to what looked like a garbage dump.[33]

The mob's decision to torture its "enemy" may have been made because there was no local authority with whom the assailants could "palaver." The hapless Bernard Mathieu was hardly the man to calm an angry mob, a mob that in ordinary circumstances would have limited itself to threats and verbal violence. Comparison with several of the incidents mentioned in Chapter 1 suggests that the intervention of a few prominent citizens and credible municipal officials would have sufficed to confine the whole affair to the realm of rhetoric.

The Bonfire, or the Makeshift Podium

At two-thirty the decision was made to burn Alain de Monéys, a form of "retaliation" perhaps suggested by the recent bonfires of Saint John.[34] The site chosen was a rundown area known locally as "the dry lake." Chambort gave instructions for building the fire. In traditional executions by burning, victims were tied to a stake, but here straw and sticks were placed on the prostrate body.[35] Roughly ten people helped prepare the bonfire, according to the estimate of Jean Frédéric, a stonecutter from Beaussac who admitted having taken part. But Chambort did most of the work. Three times he returned to the corpse with "branches from a walnut tree" that stood on the edge of the fairground. He obtained a "bundle of straw" from a tavern keeper and then added two bundles of kindling. As he worked he constantly shouted "Vive l'Empereur!"

To make sure that the fire would burn well, the fuel, along with the body beneath it, was trampled underfoot. Chambort "packed the wood down with his foot" and "danced precariously" atop the pile. According to Léonard Gauthier, young Campot also danced about and raised his arms while shouting "Vive l'Empereur!" from atop this makeshift podium.

Lighting the fire proved difficult. While Chambort ran off in search of matches, others placed scraps of old yellow paper around the base of the bonfire, next to the body. The fire, Chambort declared as the mayor looked on helplessly, should be lit by the youngest present, like the bonfires of Saint John.[36] Dubois, loyal to the end, tried in vain to prevent this final desecration. Three or four enthusiastic youths simultaneously attempted to set fire to the pile of wood and kindling. One youth whom we have encountered previously, Limay, also known as Thibassou, proved the most ardent. He struck a match on his trousers, then passed it to little Delage (Lajou), who knelt to light the paper.

The bonfire erupted into flame. According to the indictment, the men displayed a "fierce joy," and those closest to the fire fanned the flames. The execution had unleashed the crowd's Dionysiac instincts. This was no mere murder. Ordinarily murder is committed in the shadows, concealed from public view. Here, the desecration of the victim's body, the scorn, insult, and ridicule heaped upon the dead man, the joyful reaction of the crowd, and the adherence to a form of ritual (however corrupt it may have been)—all these set the execution of Alain de Monéys apart from ordinary murder, and many people were therefore aghast when it was later treated as a crime of common law.

The most vehement of the assailants scurried about the fire and harangued the crowd. On Saint John's day, men customarily displayed their oratorical prowess around the bonfire and jumped above its licking flames. The best speakers could make a name for themselves, could stand out from the crowd. Similarly, at Hautefaye, the day's events climaxed in the shadow of the flames. Renaud, who, as we have seen, addressed the assembled crowd, forcefully summed up the significance of what they had jointly accomplished.

At this point one of the few women involved in the event made her appearance. "While the body was being consumed," Philippe Dubois indicated, "people from the fair, women, children came and went and surrounded the place where this scene was taking place." The burning of the body had become part of the spectacle of the fair. "I was in the meadow," Catherine Dupuy confessed, "next to the spot where they burned Monsieur de Monéys. I saw the fire blaze up, and I could see the poor man moving under the wood piled on top of him." A butcher by the name of Laveyssière, known as Lioneau, had this to say: "On our way we stopped by the lake and saw the body . . . There were children around the blaze, and two men poked the fire." Some of the spectators inquired about the identity of the victim, proof that they had previously been involved in the activities of the fair without noticing, or at least without concerning themselves about, the progress of the murder.

Anthropologists are familiar with the style in which these people spoke around the bonfire, a style that one student of the subject has dubbed "pig talk."[37] Misinterpretation of this style was responsible for the rumors of cannibalism. Much of the imagery of the murder involved animal metaphors, an aspect of the crime that is perhaps most obvious here. The burning of the body was reminiscent not only of the bonfires of Saint John but also of the sow-burnings that were part of the usual hog-slaughter ritual. There was perhaps an even more direct connection with the practice of roasting choice parts of the pig at the time of the slaughter.[38] According to the indictment, "that night the perpetrators of this cannibalistic act told of their exploits. Some had the audacity to say that 'we roasted a fine pig in Hautefaye.'" In court Jean Bilet, a thirty-four-year-old field hand, stated that "just as the fire blazed up, Monsieur de Monéys flailed his arms and legs and made sounds like the noises a hog makes when you stick the knife into its neck." The fact that no other witness could corroborate this account only attests to the powerful hold that the image of hog slaughter exerted on the crowd's imagination.

The indictment further states that "one of them was insane enough to light his cigarette from embers taken from the body of Monsieur de Monéys. Another pointed to the body and said, 'Look how nicely it's toasting.' When Besse noticed the flaring up of the fat dripping from the body all along its length, his only regret was that all that fat was going to waste."[39] When it was all over, several men eagerly poked at the ashes and the remains of the body with their clubs.[40] During the trial, two flat stones onto which fat from the body had dripped were introduced as evidence for the prosecution.

Was Alain de Monéys still alive when the fire was lit? Was he moving? Did he feel anything when young Lajou ignited the flames? These were the questions that obsessed the court. The prosecutor skillfully harped on this emotional string. Thus, the judges were forced not only to weigh the matter of criminal responsibility but to gauge the pity of the criminals, to measure their tears, to peer into their hearts. In so doing, they disconcerted the witnesses. No one in

Hautefaye on August 16 seems to have been preoccupied with such fine estimates of the suffering inflicted.

Elie Mège, for one, claimed that "Monsieur de Monéys used his hands and feet to scatter the wood being heaped on top of him, so some of the fiercer men piled the branches back on. The victim did not have the strength to cry out." When the prosecutor asked how long Monéys might have "felt himself burning," the witness replied: "Not long. Ten or fifteen minutes." "You call that 'not long'!" the incredulous prosecutor replied. "You're heartless!" Clearly an abyss separated two systems of representing pain, two criteria, two scales of suffering. In other words, two contrasting sensibilities met in court in December 1870.

But let us return to the drama. After the body had burned, the crowd's ardor cooled and it began to reflect on the lesson of the day: "People wandered off calm and unconcerned, saying that it was a job well done and that anyone who felt pity for [Alain de Monéys] deserved the same."

Even before night fell, however, bravado slowly gave way to mounting anxiety. Yet we can learn a great deal about the significance of the event from the brief period of boasting after the deed was done. Besse, known as Deroulet, a fifty-year-old laborer, bragged to his wife that night of having poked the flames. Léonard Piarrouty prided himself "on having struck Monsieur de Monéys three times with his hook and of having gotten in four good punches." And we have already heard the boasts of those who congratulated themselves of having burned a "fine pig."

Implicit in these initial claims was the hope of monetary reward. Pierre Sarlat insisted that he and the others "were entitled to government pay." Chambort told people that he had paid a tavern keeper thirteen sous for straw for the bonfire and that he hoped to be reimbursed. François Cholet, a twenty-nine-year-old stonecutter, told Pierre Brudieu, a private guard, that he was hoping for "a reward from the emperor for burning Monsieur de Monéys." And that night, François Mazière told his employer, Madame Antony: "We did it to save France. Our emperor will surely save us."

Already, though, anxiety was beginning to silence the boasts. At the trial, Pierre Basbayou testified that Buisson had shown him a bloody stake: "He wanted to take it home as a token of his exploit. I told him he'd better throw it away, and he did so." A young girl,

Noémi, found Buisson's stake and gave it to Anne Mondout, who hastened to burn it. This proved a wise precaution, for that night the gendarmes arrived in Hautefaye to begin the investigation of what would eventually become a notorious affair. When informed of the seriousness of the incident, the chief prosecutor of the Bordeaux court decided to visit the scene himself. He arrived in Nontron on the night of the eighteenth, and the following day he went to the site of the murder.[41]

Making Sense of the Riddle

Our purpose remains to make sense of this murder and cremation. Let us begin by examining what historians have had to say about the subject of violence.

The Hautefaye tragedy does not belong to the long series of bread riots that ended in France in 1868; women traditionally played a major role in those disturbances. Nor can the Hautefaye events be seen as simply another manifestation of the latent tensions, antagonisms, and conflicts that defined the structure even as they sapped the energy of rural communities. The tragedy had nothing to do with division of communal property, interpretation of traditional easements, abuse of grazing privileges, usurpation of claims, or rights to the use of water and wood, all issues that provoked controversy and sometimes bloodshed in rural France in the nineteenth century. What happened at Hautefaye did not stem, as those issues did, from the land. Historians such as Philippe Vigier and Pierre Barral long ago examined those kinds of disturbances, the product of rural modernization and of the land hunger that continued to rack the peasantry until large-scale migration to the cities thinned its ranks.[42]

In short, it would be a mistake to search for the murder's significance in economic circumstances or to follow George Rudé's analysis of the bread-obsessed revolutionary crowd.[43] Nor was the Hautefaye crime a product of vindictive passion,[44] of the brutal settling of scores that was a constant feature of rural life.[45] When a gendarme by the name of Bidan was set upon and beaten by some thirty assailants on the square of Clamecy in December 1851, the crime could be blamed on the policeman's harsh methods.[46] But no one had anything against the young man from Bretanges, who was known only for his generosity.

The Hautefaye murder was not a part of what Raymond Verdier has called a "system of vendetta," a cycle of retribution that gives shape and pattern to outbreaks of violence.[47] Such a system can be seen at work in the series of murders that left the territory from Nîmes to Uzès stained with blood from 1790 to 1815.[48] Vendetta systems establish veritable economies of revenge in which vengeance becomes a cultural trait.[49] They involve mutual recognition, direct links between persecutor and victim, and in most cases active participation of organized youth groups. The village brawls so common in the northeastern part of the Lot region during the July Monarchy fit this description.[50] The murder of Alain de Monéys, a crime committed by grown men and without roots in a particular locality, does not.

Although agitation against taxation and the state was a fixture of life in this part of France, the murder did not stem from this well-established tradition of popular protest.[51] In 1848 and 1849 the peasants of Périgord had indeed dredged up memories of past resistance, at a time when peasants throughout Europe, squeezed by taxes destined to finance an economic takeoff, were resorting to violent forms of protest once thought to have been stamped out.[52] But in Hautefaye on August 16, 1870, no one attacked the state. On the contrary, the murderers were convinced they were doing the government's work, that they were volunteers in service of the authorities. This was no *jacquerie*, whatever contemporaries may have thought. The *jacquerie* was a venerable myth, a myth that leading citizens found so useful and frightening that they forgot the original meaning of the term. The image purveyed by the novel *Jacquou le Croquant* was a distortion of the reality. Its author based his account on stories from many different periods, from which he drew freely. The most one can say is that the Hautefaye criminals treated their victim's body in the same way that other bodies had been treated in the past.

The peasants at the fair had made no attempt to mimic the procedures of popular justice. In this respect the execution of Alain de Monéys differed radically from the September Massacres carried out in Paris in 1792. The cruel procession in which the young noble from Bretanges was made to march was by no means a tragic carnival. It did not exhibit those comic aspects of popular culture that Mikhail Bakhtin has described.[53] Derision played little part in the execution of the crime.[54] There were none of the signs of hierarchical inversion that accompanied the murder of Chambert, the usurer of Buzançais, on January 13, 1847. There was no attack on the social order and none of the carnival's social intensity. No one in Hautefaye wore a disguise; no one masqueraded as a lord. There was no banter or playacting. To be sure, the victim was in a sense nothing more than a dummy, like those whose cremation traditionally marked the end of revels, the farewell ceremony. But any resemblance to a carnival ends there.

What was going on then? On August 16, 1870, the peasants on the fairground at Hautefaye were attempting to exorcise the fear that held them in its grip, attempting to ward off an imminent disaster. Dreadfully certain that their homes would be sacked and burned if the emperor fell victim to treason, they were quick to burn the "Prussian" in their midst.

Those present on the fairground believed that the emperor's three internal enemies were united in a conspiracy.[55] If the Prussians lurking within French borders could be eliminated at a time when the country's men were marching off to war, the danger of being surprised from the rear would also be eliminated. In this respect the Hautefaye crime was a reprise of the events of the summer of 1792: not the September Massacres in Paris but the bloody murders that took place in the provinces in July and August, of which Pierre Caron has catalogued sixty-five.[56] In one *département*, Orne, studied by Paul Nicolle, massacres occurred in eight different communes.[57] The situation that Périgord peasants believed to exist on August 16, 1870, was admittedly somewhat different. The emperor, they thought, was defending France against invasion, whereas republicans had joined nobles and priests in an obscure plot against the nation.

Yet even allowing for that difference, the degree to which some of the slogans shouted on the Hautefaye fairground in 1870 echoed those of the summer of 1792 or of July 1815 is striking. The hog dealer Desvars heard someone say that "the nobility and the curés are the reason our children are leaving" for war. The butcher Laveyssière reported that "as the victim was being put to torture" some of his assailants began screaming that "all aristocrats must be killed." According to François Campot, some people charged that Monéys had shouted "Vive la République!" "These words angered the young men who had been called to serve, who wanted to defend the emperor," Campot testified. (Remember that the trial took place under a republican government.) When François Bordas, a "land-lord," accused Léonard Piarrouty of unwarranted cruelty, the rag-picker replied that "noble scoundrels like him" were "responsible for my son's now lying in perhaps a thousand pieces." The accusa-tion at Reichshoffen and the massacre at Hautefaye, separated by two weeks, were somehow symmetrical. In this sense, but only in this sense, the murder can be described as a crime of vengeance.

The Hautefaye affair therefore was not, as some republican leaders claimed, an episode in a "reactive revolution." In some ways it was a continuation of a pattern that can be traced back to the Revolution. The man the peasants tortured was a symbol of the much-hated Little Vendée. Thus the tragedy was in one sense an anachronistic resurgence of the horror of revolution.

But that is by no means all there was to it. The torture of Alain de Monéys was above all an affirmation of identity. Smallholding peasants, dispersed throughout a region whose rural hamlets appear to have lacked cohesion, saw the fair as an opportunity to celebrate the life they shared.[58] Far from the town of Nontron with its prom-inent citizens and government officials, Hautefaye was an ideal place for peasants to meet, enjoy one another's company, and trade ru-mors.

The people who gathered for a short while on and around the fairground of Hautefaye found it easier to talk politics there than anywhere else. They could openly voice their political views and even translate them into political acts. And they could celebrate their loyalty to the sovereign and his dynasty without fear of ridicule. The Hautefaye murder was a cry of love to an imperiled emperor.[59] Republicans, moreover, were not mistaken about what that cry meant. Its ferocity was a reponse to the gravity of the situation, and its urgency reflected the peasants' isolation now that "enlightened Bonapartists" in the towns had abandoned the cause.[60]

If we look beyond the august[61] personage of the emperor, we see that the torture of Alain de Monéys is one sign of a sudden intensification of nationalist sentiment earlier in the month. As ran-cor over the republican opposition's rhetoric turned to outright enmity, peasants dreamed that the entire nation would suddenly coalesce in opposition to the invader.

One aim of the murder was to forge this coalition of national defense.[62] The mob on the fairground that day was an unstable, temporary congregation. It was not a village fortified by age-old allegiances and paradoxically invigorated by its tensions, nor was it a community in which people knew one another and shared common interests. Everyone who moved along the narrow paths of Hautefaye that day was required to strike a blow against Monéys, and the same fate was promised to anyone foolish enough to stand up for him. Jubilation erupted around the fire as the body of the "enemy" burned.

The violence got out of hand. The enormity of the event stems not so much from its brutality as from the deliberate blindness of the murderers. Although the assailants in some sense "knew" that their victim was a local noble, they refused to acknowledge his identity, to concede the obvious. Their need to strike at the enemy overwhelmed their judgment. Some historians, rather too hasty to follow Georges Lefebvre in his fondness for crowd psychology, have therefore suggested mass delusion as an explanation.[63]

Who can deny that mass delusion did play a part? The secret of the crime lies not in the victim's actual identity but in his perceived identity in the eyes of his attackers. The torture victim was a mere prop, a pretext for a larger purpose, just as the scene of the crime encompassed an area far wider than the tiny commune of Hautefaye. On the fairground and along the byways of the commune, "unavowable and irresolvable tensions" were projected onto the innocent victim.[64] The disorderly mob was out to regain some control over its destiny by simplifying the situation, compressing all its troubles into a single confrontation. Therein, perhaps, lies the ultimate key to actions that have remained enigmatic to this day. René Girard's analysis of the mechanics of victimization comes to mind.[65] The crowd gathered on the fairground had, to borrow Girard's terms, "an absolute conviction that it had found the single cause of its woes" and "a reassuring certainty of its adversary's identity, [his] abominable difference" from themselves.[66]

The Périgord murderers hoped to expel the monster from their midst, to purify the community by ridding it of a man who was at once a noble, an ally of the curés, a republican, and a Prussian. After the fact, they were seen as the very incarnation of the most abominable of monsters, the very "cannibals" of whom France had been seeking to rid itself since the first days of the Revolution.

But the most important historical fact about the Hautefaye

crime has yet to be considered: its incongruity with the political culture of the time. An act that as late as 1792 could still be considered an acceptable, even a noble, expression of public opinion could, in August 1870, inspire nothing but horror in observers from every part of the political spectrum. The sensibility of the nation had changed. The rest of French society looked at the Hautefaye assailants with utter incredulity. At the same time, of course, society projected its own fantasies onto the alleged "cannibals."

4

Monstrous Brutes

❧

"Monadnock" is a word that comes to mind to describe the killing of Alain de Monéys. Geographers use the term to refer to an isolated hill or mountain of resistant rock that juts up from a surrounding plain as witness to the geological past. The chief interest of the Hautefaye tragedy lies in its aura of strangeness. During the trial in Périgueux, the chief judge expressed the peculiarity of the "heinous crime" in a striking phrase: it was tantamount, he said, to a denial of the nineteenth century.

For historical anthropologists the event therefore provides a promising approach to the study of important social processes. The Hautefaye tragedy is fascinating because it reveals a gap between the sensibility of the majority and that of at least one small group of isolated peasants, whose behavior apparently was unaffected by changes in what the rest of society deemed tolerable. It is this gap that makes the murder historically interesting. The crime is important only because of its late date. Had the tragedy occurred any time between the fourteenth century and 1795, it would have faded into insignificance. Indeed, it would have stood out only for the relative mildness of the cruelty visited upon the victim.

Accordingly, it makes sense now to shift our attention from the crime itself to how it was perceived, to the reasons it struck contemporaries as so bizarre. The horror and anger, disbelief and stupefaction that greeted the event suggest how rapidly things had changed since the end of the Revolution. The point is worth elaborating more fully, and to do so I shall embark on a lengthy digression, in the course of which I shall refer to several magnificent recent books.

Together these works surely constitute one of the most remarkable historiographic achievements of the past decade.[1]

Massacres have been common in modern times. Emmanuel Le Roy Ladurie, Frank Lestringant, and Denis Crouzet, in studying behavior of such unspeakable cruelty that it is now considered beyond the pale of civilization, have given us new insight into the importance of cannibalistic images and practices.[2] While the anthropologist may distinguish between "siege cannibalism," "famine cannibalism," "vendetta cannibalism," and "criminal cannibalism," all of these cause us to recoil in horror. Yet anyone with a taste for history as it really was cannot help being haunted by any number of barbaric episodes: the "endogenous cannibalism" of mothers in Sancerre who devoured their children; the killers who ate the livers of the Huguenots they murdered; the fricasees of human ears and grilled hearts that were served up during the Saint Bartholomew massacres; the auctions of human flesh in the city of Romans in 1580; and the abominable acts committed in besieged Paris in 1589.

The significance of these heinous crimes cannot be understood without reference to their symbolic and religious connotations. For the men and women of the sixteenth century, cannibalism was more than just a dreadful crime; it was also symptomatic "of a disruption of the order of the universe." In a world rich in divine prodigies and signs and tormented by eschatological obsessions, religious symbolism melded image with reality.

The Catholic side in the sixteenth-century Wars of Religion remains unsurpassed in its zeal for religious massacre. According to Denis Crouzet, acts of religious violence proceeded in three stages: first, desecrate the body and drag it from place to place; second, stone it; third, burn it.[3] Each stage had multiple meanings. The first revealed the loathesomeness of the victim. "The ritual of violence explores the innermost recesses of the body" in order to wrest the hideous idol from its envelope of flesh.[4] Vital organs were therefore plucked from the corpse.

Even as the attackers dehumanized their victims, they bore witness to the sacred purpose of their act. "Bestial violence" may have revealed the animal in man,[5] but it also made possible "contemplation of the Lord's miraculous wrath, which left its mark on the corpse that served as its theater."[6] Mayhem prefigured the imagined violence of hell. Massacres were literally a theatricalization of damnation. The disfigurement of the dead, the mutilation of corpses by ravenous dogs, anticipated the torture of the damned.

Violence was also significant in many other ways. It could be a festive act or part of a ritual of propitiation or purification.[7] Sometimes its purpose was to appease God's wrath. Other times it was nothing more than a political act. The Saint Bartholomew Massacres grew out of a desire to put heretics to death; but as things got out of hand, the violence increasingly turned toward dramatizing the eternal torment that allegedly awaited apostates from the Catholic faith.

From 1580 until about 1594, Europeans experienced a growing "horror of self."[8] Many people were convinced that enlightened Christians were closer to savage cannibals than they had once believed. Violence turned inward and assumed ever more fantastic forms as Dionysiac impulses were channeled into the imagination rather than into the outside world. Mayhem turned literary. Later, in the Wars of Religion, the field of carnage moved from the city to the battlefield, and cruelty took new forms. These were important changes, and I shall have more to say about them when I take up the period from 1792 to 1851. In some ways the Revolution simply repeated the Wars of Religion.

The shift from actual to imaginary violence was perhaps a consequence of the guilt that actual violence inspired. Norbert Elias's account of the civilizing process (a progressive increase of self-discipline and internalization of norms) offers a somewhat different light on the phenomenon. The change is consistent, moreover, with Lucien Febvre's claim that outwardly emotional behavior declined over the course of the sixteenth century. Denis Crouzet, for his part, sees the shift as a prelude to the triumph of modern rationality over postmedieval magic and superstition.[9]

Yet highly symbolic forms of vengeance and "ceremonial mutilation" of bodies were by no means unknown in the seventeenth and eighteenth centuries.[10] It is important to note that the people who took part in massacres were not primarily interested in torturing their victims; ritual violence was directed mainly against corpses. Bodies were frequently stripped and castrated; faces were mutilated, eyes plucked out, limbs chopped off, heads severed. Angry mobs dragged corpses face down toward rivers or sewers. Burial was not allowed. Severed heads, limbs, and genitals were paraded about in noisy processions and exhibited as trophies.

At the same time, legal executions were conducted according to a "sacrificial system."[11] The purpose of brutal execution rituals was not only to profane or execrate the victim but also to expiate and purify. Torturing a criminal wiped away the sacrilege of his crime. It was a sacrifice that marked a reconciliation with God, a reinstatement in society through the purifying, regenerative power of spilled blood. Torment converted murder into a means of salvation. It expressed the hope that an unfeeling monster might be transformed into a martyr, a vicious thief into a luminous saint whose bloody relics would be fought over by onlookers.

The scene of torture was a place sanctified by the spilling of impure blood. Those who watched found themselves momentarily united by the solemnity of the spectacle. A fairground or market square (as in Caen in 1760, where the crowd included women and children) could thus become a temporary holy place. Spectators came there to experience the victim's agony, to contemplate "the grand act of dying in public torment."[12] Executions were also occasions for celebration. People gambled, drank, and brawled in the shadow of the gallows. Minutely orchestrated, torture played on a well-tempered scale of emotions.

Over time, however, these scenes of mass murder and torture inspired growing feelings of horror, which ultimately undermined the coherence of the associated rituals. The inventiveness and variety of the acts of mayhem slowly diminished.[13] Certain sensitive souls found unbearable the eleven hours of torment inflicted on the would-be regicide Damiens.[14] The curiosity of the crowd came to seem unspeakably cruel. In short, the humanitarianism of the Enlightenment did its work. A new sensibility arose, a new dismay in the face of ancient rituals of torture and mayhem.

Sensitive souls, reacting to pain in a new way, began to fear suffering as never before.[15] Humanitarian discourse painted a novel image of man, first in fiction and theater but later, as we know from dissection notes, in medicine as well.[16] Meanwhile, everyday life lost something of its sacred character. The concept of sacrilege was challenged, attenuated, and eventually repudiated. Sacrificial torture was reviled and massacre denounced as horrifying. Thus drained of meaning, the two chief forms of ritual violence became obsolete.

Once the connection between massacre and the sacred was severed, massacre became an offense to sensitive souls, an outrageous crime. The spectator steeped in the Enlightenment spirit felt keenly the anthropological distance between himself and the violent mob. Men suddenly became aware of what was exorbitant in man, hence in themselves. In short, the spectacle of violence inspired horror.[17] The enlightened individual recoiled from the abjection of his fellow human beings, felt revulsion at the threatening proximity of bestiality. The scandal of massacre lay not so much in the spilling of blood as in the unmediated production of corpses without order or system of any kind. Unlike torture, whose traditional rituals were tenaciously maintained, massacre devolved into chaos and futility, a frenzy in a vacuum. Harrowed by fear, the eighteenth century cringed as never before at the sight of sudden death.[18]

Massacre, the sight of massacre, and the narration of massacre gave sensitive souls a keen new awareness of social difference. Violent men were found to be revoltingly similar to animals. The mob was a bloodthirsty beast, a vile human swamp. Murderous mobs were compared to what they produced: dead meat, disgusting excrement.

Some people now began to argue that the sight of horror was apt to produce depravity and pervert the senses.[19] Criticism of torture and of the death penalty began early in the century. The monster was turned inside out. The body, now safe from physical torment, became an object of scientific investigation.[20] Michel Foucault has shown how a new penal system was developed. Methods of execution were also modified.

In this change of sensibility the Revolution played an important part. A theater of massacre and torture on a vast scale, the Revolution occurred just as the sacrificial system was beginning to break down, hastening its obsolescence. Old forces of violence and mayhem were unleashed at a time when torture and massacre had become intolerable to people of enlightened sensibility.

The watershed year was 1792.[21] Joyous carnage proceeded even as it was denounced by those for whom such violence had become unacceptable. In each of Caron's sixty-five instances of mass murder in the provinces, we note the reappearance of ancient ritual forms of massacre. The most astute student of the process, Bernard Conein, offers some illuminating examples.[22] Murder and desecration by angry mobs horrified sensitive souls desperate to make sense of the sudden outbreak of blind, anonymous violence in a society suddenly deprived of its key symbols.[23]

On July 22, 1789, a soldier held up "a bloody bit of flesh" in front of the Hôtel de Ville in Paris and declared, "This is Bertier's heart!" One witness wrote that "we looked away, and he was forced to withdraw."[24] Similar confrontations throughout France revealed the glaring contrast of new and old sensibilities.

In 1792 mass murderers reveled in crimes they shamelessly confessed to the authorities. One man who had participated in the murder of the comte de Saillans wrote to the municipality of Largentière on July 12. The "monster" and his companions, he said, "were killed in fine fashion, decapitated. We have the heads. Tournett had the honor of striking first, and never was an execution more pleasant or agreeable! The leaders asked that they be handed over to the courts, but like banshees we all screamed, 'No courts! No prison!'"[25]

Yet many found what Pétion called the "field of carnage" unbearable to behold. Orators sought to teach their audiences the language of justice and humanity, but the "frenzied populace" could not or would not listen. Describing his own actions at the Abbaye in 1792, Manuel said: "Standing atop a pile of bodies, I preached respect for the Law."[26]

On September 9 and 10, 1792, there was a massacre of prisoners in Orléans. The mayor, unable to stem the anger of the mob, was left speechless by the spectacle of horror: "He tried to speak, but sobs choked his voice. He covered his eyes, but someone grabbed him. He saw the massacre, lost consciousness, was carried into a house, came to, wanted to leave, was restrained, said that although there were men who dishonored themselves, he hoped to die for the Law . . . He went out and a spectacle of horror greeted all his senses. Blood, death, plaintive cries, dreadful screams, severed limbs."[27] These words, taken from his affidavit, are the best evidence we have of just how terrifying it could be to be suddenly confronted with one's distance from other human beings.

By the end of 1792, however, the popular forms of public

execution began to vanish from the scene; sanctified and tragic forms of torture gave way to a "secularized and moralistic system of [social] utility."[28] Daniel Arasse has written a masterly study of the new forms of execution.[29] The guillotine, which made prompt justice possible, satisfied the desires of the sans-culottes. Assembly-line executions supplanted the older forms of massacre.[30] Most important of all, the "austere blade" reflected the new attitude toward pain. Efficient and instantaneous in its operation, the guillotine administered death without suffering, or so it was thought.[31] Torment and agony were no longer drawn out in a lengthy spectacle. Execution was drained of its sacred significance. The corrupting effects of executions on spectators were avoided. Shorn of excess, the administration of death became an edifying spectacle. Repentance was still possible. Indeed, a literature of last words flourished.[32] The time previously filled with the making of the martyr was now devoted to *ante mortem* discourse. In fact, it proved to be not at all easy to separate death from the sacred, which wormed its way into the interstices of the new ritual—but that is another story.

After the winter of 1792 (and leaving aside the cruel barbarity of the Vendée War of 1793), mob violence declined throughout France even as the mechanism of the Terror was being put in place.[33] To be sure, the "frenzied populace" had not quite reached the end of its rampage. But after Thermidor the new sensibility began to take hold. In retrospect, people began to describe the violent mobs of years past as "cannibals."[34] Tales of bloodthirsty violence began to appear in the summer of 1794, the first of an endless flood of writing that conjured up the specter of such bloody tyrants as Caligula, Nero, Caracalla, and Heliogabalus, the better to smite the "monsters" of the Revolution with the bludgeon of public disapproval. The lengthy martyrology compiled at this time in both the revolutionary and counterrevolutionary camps would leave indelible traces on the national memory.

To take just one example, L. M. Prudhomme took it upon himself to "set frightening portraits of butchery" before "the reader's distraught soul."[35] He made it his duty to "root about in this foul sewer of horrors of every description," much as Parent-Duchâtelet would soon root about in the actual sewers of the capital.[36] The enterprising author dredged up the worst crimes, among them the murder of Belzunce in Caen on August 11, 1789, which Prudhomme described as a sort of epilogue to the Saint Bartholomew Massacres and the torture and execution of Ravaillac: "His body was dismembered. His head was placed atop a stick and carried about, as had been done in Paris. But something happened in Caen that had not been seen in the capital: many citizens wanted a shred of his flesh. Some took pieces home in their pockets. Others saw to it that the head was preceded by a pike beribboned with the victim's entrails. One man, or, rather, savage, sent a chunk of flesh off to a bakery to be baked for a family meal. One midwife went even further: she did not rest until she had obtained a piece of the victim's genitals, which she kept in a jar filled with wine spirits."[37] Images of savagery had become an obsession. Understanding such images is an important clue to nineteenth-century political attitudes.

Of particular interest in this regard are the riot of Prairial, Year III (of the revolutionary calendar), and the decapitation of the unfortunate Féraud, whose head was paraded around the Convention for hours on end. Féraud's death was in fact the first ritual murder (or "massacre" of a single victim) to be described as an anachronistic resurgence of primitive "cannibalism." It appears to have been the first collective murder to arouse the kind of indignation that the Hautefaye affair aroused, including the denunciation of the crime as "bizarre."

Careful analysis of the White Terror reveals how rapid the evolution was. Mob behavior in 1815 owed little to the traditional ritual code. Few corpses were dismembered, in contrast to 1792. Body parts were not exhibited as trophies. A few bodies were desecrated, Marshal Brune's among them. In the Nîmes-Uzès region the White Terror had more in common with the violence of robbers out for vengeance or booty than with the Terror of 1792. In Toulouse, the cruel treatment of General Ramel by the *verdets* was more torture than massacre.[38]

Between the return of the Bourbons and the Périgord incident, sensitivity to these issues continued to increase. As more modern attitudes toward pain gained currency, they simultaneously acquired new depth.[39] Following the teachings of the Idéologues, and especially Cabanis, people became accustomed to looking more closely at their feelings.[40] A person attuned to his own bodily twinges and to the murmur of his organs was apt to take a dim view of inflicting pain on others. But these changes affected different segments of society at different rates, so that anthropological differences developed within French society.

Analgesic techniques progressed steadily in the early decades of the nineteenth century. Then, in 1846, anesthesia was administered for the first time.[41] People consequently became less tolerant of pain, and their fear of suffering increased.

Memories of pain and bloodletting gradually faded from all strata of society. Animal slaughter, banished from downtown areas and retail butcher shops, was increasingly hidden from view.[42] It was forbidden to spill animal blood in city streets. The transportation of carcasses was regulated. On the basis of such regulations, imperial authorities declared the meatpacking industry to be no threat to the public health.[43] The "connection between bloody death and meat" was hidden. The sacrificial and festive trappings that had traditionally surrounded the slaughter of animals gradually disappeared. In 1833 a law was passed prohibiting animal fights inside the city limits of Paris. In 1850 the Grammont Law outlawed violence against animals in public.[44]

At around this time the last vestiges of torture were eliminated from the criminal justice system. The branding of convicts with a red-hot iron was abolished in 1832. The public display of criminals was outlawed in 1848. The only remaining public punishment was execution by guillotine.[45] In 1832, however, the site of executions in Paris was moved from the neighborhood of the Hôtel de Ville, centrally located close to the Seine, to the remote *Saint-Jacques* customs gate.

These proliferating signs of humanitarian concern were accompanied, as Philippe Ariès has noted, by a new desire to honor the dead.[46] The corpse became an object of respect.[47] Yet fascination with the macabre remained strong. Throughout the nineteenth century, visits to morgues remained a popular pastime.[48] But this was the only hitch in the otherwise unimpeded rise of the new sensibility vis-à-vis suffering, sickness, death, and decay.

Violence, it is commonly said, was on the decline throughout the nineteenth century. Voltaire, in *Le siècle de Louis XIV,* had predicted that violence would eventually disappear from the face of the earth. Modern scholars from Norbert Elias to Richard Tilly have analyzed and interpreted the attenuation of violence in a variety of ways.[49] I think it would be wise, however, to inject a note of caution into the discussion. Violence certainly did not disappear. What did happen was that people increasingly became intolerant of the legibility *(lisibilité)* of public cruelty.[50] Public cruelty not only persisted but probably became more common than ever, yet its appearance changed. The nineteenth century was a century of great carnage, of vast battlefields and lethal repression: between 1,700 and 3,000 people died in Paris in June 1848; between 20,000 and 25,000 died in May 1871. Yet mob violence was less acceptable than ever before. People insisted that the authorities protect them in the streets and safeguard them in their homes, and accordingly felt revulsion at the bewildering spectacle of mob violence, with its terrifying prospect of sudden death. The mob was a monster, and as such to be expunged from society.

The unleashing of the incomprehensible and blind forces of massacre came to be seen as unacceptable and even obscene, in the proper sense of the word—the equivalent of public displays of nudity or hog slaughtering in city streets. Although 1792 was still fresh in memory, the past receded rapidly; its ferocity came to seem incomprehensible. Nineteenth-century men and women found the cruelty of past generations bizarre and astonishing. "Only another people, another civilization, could have behaved that way," or so it was said.[51] Pierre Rétat, speaking of the torture of Damiens, asserted that "the nineteenth century stakes its claim to dignity on the categorical rejection of such ancestors." Outrage at stories of torture and massacre "arises more out of the proximity of the event than the nature of the crime."

As the nineteenth century progressed, people sought to distance themselves from the violence of the past, to affirm the alien nature of barbarous acts whose strange proximity made a powerful impression, to forget that the sight of bloodshed and torture had only recently inspired no revulsion in ordinary people. On December 7, 1831, the republican Armand Carrel wrote that "it was of great importance to us that history repeated itself, demonstrating that the *peuple* of 1791, so sluggish in its intelligence, . . . [and] the murderous populace of 1793 . . . are now two centuries behind us."[52] The militant democrat cannot believe that nothing distinguishes the *peuple* of 1789 and 1792, which bludgeoned Foulon and murdered Carmes, from the fraternal crowd that took part in the Festival of the Federation.

Throughout the nineteenth century it was common to exaggerate the hideous features of mob violence in order to exorcise the specter of Dionysiac instincts unleashed. Thus, fear of cannibalism became increasingly common as people accentuated the anthropological distance between themselves and their recent ancestors, who inhabited what Edgar Quinet once called the "desert of dread." The new sensibility only magnified the horror. The recounting of Damiens's torture provides an interesting index of the change: during the Second Empire the judicial aspects of the procedure were played down, leaving nothing but "the hideous spectacle of torture."[53] Similarly, Georges Benrekassa has shown how Marat's image was blackened over the years.[54] During the July Monarchy the "friend of the people" was portayed as a sewer-dwelling reptile. A bloodthirsty, nocturnal, scum-vomiting beast, Marat eventually became the symbol of the torchbearing rabble. The *Journal des débats* for July 19, 1847, warned: "Do not trifle with such crimes. Do not toy with such axes. Do not stir still-smoldering fires . . . Silence! The tiger is not slain; it crouches in its lair. Do not awaken it, lest it devour you."[55] It would be several more decades before the Marat legend would forsake teratology in favor of mental pathology.

One consequence of the new sensibility was that people became afraid of the ruthless cruelty of what they called the "rabble." This anxiety was heightened by social imagery that was based less on actual danger than on feelings of radical anthropological difference. Many believed that it was difficult for anyone born into the lower orders, the "infinity below," to develop truly as an individual, to become fully human.[56]

There were many strategies for coping with this social fear. One was to try to confine it within the limits of the imagination. This compensatory strategy has been analyzed by Mario Praz and other specialists in the literature of horror and sadism.[57] Fewer scholars, unfortunately, have looked into new ways of improving security and new approaches to law and order.[58] General Bonaparte's suppression of the Vendémiaire insurrection, for example, exemplifies the "modern" form of urban carnage, perpetrated by troops armed with rifles and artillery.[59]

The nineteenth-century form of mass killing, the response to obsessive fears of frenzied mob violence, was a disciplined affair, inspired by images borrowed from the battlefield. Death was now instantaneous. It had shed those traits that once linked it to torture. Its ritual was simplified. Its narration became elliptical. Its traces were quickly erased. This new, permissible, understated form of bloodbath was calming and reassuring. Too little attention has been paid to the fundamental importance of mass killing in nineteenth-century French history. The violent events of 1831–1835, June 1848, December 1851, and May 1871 have rightly been perceived and analyzed as episodes in a single revolutionary process. The crushing of mass movements has been interpreted as a manifestation of re-pressive will and nothing more. Yet it is as if no regime could establish itself firmly until it had proved its capacity to bathe in the blood of the monster: the angry populace, the frenzied mob. There is a tendency to forget that mass killing had other purposes besides repression. It could also calm tensions and restore social harmony after periods of turmoil.[60] Hence it would be misleading to claim that collective violence diminished in the nineteenth century. Gov-ernments appear to have acted as they did in order to quell social fear, by which I mean the horror felt by the dominant class owing to its anthropological distance from a threatening Other.

But there were other ways of exorcising nightmarish memories and fears of repetition. In the wake of Thermidor, plans were made to "civilize" the common man, to change his nature radically.[61] Nineteenth-century authorities clung firmly to this worthy educa-tional goal. Many attempts were made to paint "good" citizens as heroes, thus casting all who did not conform to the model as "bad."[62] Louis Chevalier has argued that the "laborious" classes of society were also regarded as "dangerous" classes; this thesis should be read in the light of various procedures by which a new line was drawn between the good *peuple*—hardworking, healthy, moral, and generous—and the bad.[63] Consider, for example, various mythical figures of the common man that were proposed between the summer of 1830 and the spring of 1832. David Pinkney and others[64] have traced the government's efforts to cast the people of July in a heroic light. Ten years after the insurrection its heroes were buried beneath a column in the place de la Bastille.[65] The martyrs of liberty were rewarded with medals, crosses, and other tokens of esteem. Yet a few months later the same government characterized the populace of the *faubourgs* as a horde of atavistic savages laying siege to an imperiled city. The moment the common man failed to live up to what was expected of him, his image reverted to that of a primitive savage.

In February 1848, victims of a fusillade on the boulevard des Capucines were spontaneously transformed into heroes and placed on display, provoking a rebellion of working people and a segment of the bourgeoisie on the night of February 23–24.[66] When this coalition fell apart a few months later, however, the rebellious people of June, the *peuple* whom Tocqueville saw as a throwback to the rebellious slaves of antiquity, would be massacred in their turn. This new bloodletting followed interminable discussions and outward expressions of fraternity that were also attempts to lay the ghost of social fear.[67]

In December 1851 in Clamecy, socialist-democrat leaders, members of the petite bourgeoisie, discovered to their astonishment that the insurgent troops they were leading had, through the murder of a gendarme named Bidan, metamorphosed into their leaders' worst nightmare: a frenzied mob.[68] One could easily cite many examples of similarly dramatic changes of representation, as decisive as actual changes in the social composition of insurgent ranks.

Since 1871 most historical works have tended to play down the violence in nineteenth-century events. The substance has been systematically drained from the postrevolutionary period. Carnage has been glossed over. The blood of revolution has been carefully washed away, leaving only the diaphanous halo of the martyr.[69]

This fear of soiling the pages of history with the stuff of reality distinguishes nineteenth-century historians from their colleagues, and it is important to understand its significance and function. Fastidious and fearful historians appear to have conspired with the men of the time to cover up horrific events. We know virtually nothing about murderous nineteenth-century mobs and very little about lethal tactics of law enforcement. Historical narrative has been watered down and cruelty banished from its pages. Historians have behaved as though the only reason for studying mob violence were to ascertain the poverty of the crowd, its possible role in the revolutionary process, and its level of political consciousness.

History written in this prim and proper way has been obsessed with the need to distinguish sharply between the good and the wicked and thus, paradoxically, has led to an uncritical confounding of unrelated massacres. The history of representations has consequently been decapitated. Attempts to trace the evolution of collective sensibilities have been rejected out of hand. Every effort to reconstruct the true aspect of horror and the actual practice of cruelty has been blocked.

Let us return to the post-Thermidor representation of mob violence. Although "cannibalism" was an obsessive concern, the subject cannot be explored in any detail here.[70] Jean-Pierre Peter long ago searched the Restoration archives for ogres who were alleged to have eaten their own flesh and blood.[71] Court records of the period are a veritable chamber of horrors. The abominable crime of Pierre Rivière caused a major stir.[72] The cannibals on the "raft of the *Medusa*" were for a time an object of horrifed fascination.[73] Prefects fulminated endlessly against "savage hordes" and against the "barbarous habits" of the dreadful Lot peasants whose children slaughtered one another.[74] In 1832, at the height of the cholera epidemic, mobs in Paris accused innocent bystanders of poisoning the population and bludgeoned them to death; horrified onlookers saw in these crimes the resurrection of ancient demons.[75] Jewish homes in Alsace were sacked following the establishment of the Republic.[76] In June 1848 mobile guardsmen were placed between two boards and sawed in half. These bloody events fed the nightmares of the bourgeoisie. In December 1851 Parisian rumormongers turned the Clamecy insurrection into a veritable saturnalia. Viel-Castel assures us that people in Princess Mathilde's entourage discussed the alleged rape of thirty-eight young women by a gang of venerially infected men in a scene witnessed by horrified priests tied to stakes before being tortured.[77] The catalogue of nineteenth-century horrors is still far from complete, and one day it will need to be studied in depth. In short, the interpretation of the Hautefaye crime—or for that matter of the massacre on the rue Haxo, of the stories of violent acts committed by the *pétroleuses* (incendiaries of 1871), of the tales of beautiful women poking out the eyes of Commune prisoners with the sharpened points of their parasols—belongs to a history of cruel acts and a logic of social imagery that cannot be elucidated without help from cultural anthropology.

But that is for the future. Already we can see that the Hautefaye event is exceptionally rich in meaning. On the fairground of that Nontronnais village, the phantoms of cannibals rubbed shoulders with the ghosts of "Jacques." Yet contemporary images of mob violence tended to emphasize mob psychology rather than atavistic freaks. The monster that emerged from the past at Hautefaye thus seemed exceedingly strange. In an age of massacre on a vast scale, this one act of torture baffled all attempts at exorcism. The crime revealed Dionysiac instincts believed to have been forever laid to rest, thus compounding its horror.

The Charred Statue

When such ghosts from the past reemerged, political differences ceased to matter. Society cringed as one at this reminder of the terrifying side of human nature. The response to the crime was immediate, and it was one of absolute horror, even if the dreadful carnage of the war, anguish over the Prussian siege, and stories of sharpshooters burned alive at Châteaudun resulted in a somewhat muted public outcry. Republicans, meanwhile, found themselves at a loss. Still, the strange metamorphosis of good peasants into ruthless monsters was a spectacle that many people found utterly fascinating.

The August 20 issue of *Le Nontronnais* contained a description of those "monsters" that many of them may have read. They were called "cannibals," "drunk on blood," "a brutish mob," "creatures with human faces" who dared set fire to a fellow human being, an "atrocious crime that takes us right back to the *jacqueries* of the Middle Ages." The evening before, another newspaper, *Le Charentais,* had denounced, in a fantastic account of the event, what it called a "dreadful crime," an "atrocious act of barbary," and "scenes of savagery." On August 23 the official *Moniteur* condemned "the horror" of the torture. For Alcide Dusolier, the people involved were nothing less than "savages."[78] In one *complainte* (an already old-fashioned ballard form), the political crime of Hautefaye was treated on the model of remarkable individual crimes of the past: throughout the fall of 1870 people sang, to the "tune of Fualdès," of the "sad horrors" perpetrated in the Dordogne village.[79]

Reaction to the crime did not end with invective, however. The true horror of the mob's behavior was subjected to careful scrutiny. Unlike the massacres at Buzançais and Clamecy, the Périgord murder revived ancient forms of torture. Romantic literature delighted in nocturnal crimes and shadowy monsters, but the shocking barbarity at Hautefaye had been committed in broad daylight. The horror of the crime was beyond imagination. Charles Ponsac wrote that "the murder of Fualdès was more mysterious than that of Monsieur de Monéys, but that is its only advantage. It was certainly less dreadful and terrifying. What makes the murder of Monsieur de Monéys more sinister is the fact that it was committed out of doors under clear skies."[80] Society was quick to forget that peasant violence in central France had traditionally occurred in daylight hours, when spectators were most numerous.[81]

The atmosphere surrounding the murder was exuberant. "As in *Robinson Crusoe*, the cannibals" danced around the body, while the mayor, symbol of subverted authority, watched helplessly. The assailants showed no respect for their victim, whom they treated in degrading ways, like an animal. On February 13, 1871, *L'Echo de la Dordogne* reminded its readers that the peasants of Hautefaye had "roasted" poor Monsieur de Monéys "like a filthy animal."

The literature inspired by the event aimed not to move but to horrify its readers. Dr. Roby-Pavillon, who performed the autopsy on August 16, wrote a report that is a striking example of how easily the "realism" of scientific language could be contaminated by the fancy of "humanitarian" discourse. Here is his description of the pitiful body: "The corpse, charred almost beyond recognition, was lying on its back, the face slightly turned to the left toward the sky, its lower limbs spread apart, the right hand clenched above the head as if to implore, the left hand drawn down toward the left shoulder and open, as if begging for mercy. The features of the face expressed pain; the torso was twisted and drawn to the rear. This was the attitude in which the flames caught Alain de Monéys and preserved his body for the court, as if to express the suffering of his final moments."[82]

After the autopsy, the "statue" was wrapped in two bedsheets in the presence of the victim's mother and of his brother, the abbé de Monéys. The charred remains were then carried into the church "on the dead men's litter." That night they were placed in a coffin and the next day buried at Beaussac.

The horror only compounded the fear felt by the region's aristocrats. On August 22 the victim's uncle wrote to Jules de Verneilh, a local noble, that his daughter had "wrested all the Monéis [sic] of Bretanges from the hands of those cannibals and placed them in the

protective custody of the Bordeaux court."[83] In the immediate vicinity of Hautefaye, the Monéys, Saint-Cyrs, Conans, and Bellussières,
aided by neighbors, friends, servants, and tenant farmers, had
mounted a defense on the night of the crime.[84] The August 20 issue
of *Le Nontronnais* alluded to abortive attacks on certain country
houses but gave no further details. Note that the most resolute of
the murderers on the night of August 16 had no intention of stop-
ping with the death of Monéys.[85]

The ghost of "Jacques" would haunt the aristocracy for a long
time to come. On May 7, 1872, Monsieur de Lasfond, owner of the
château of Poutignac, wrote Mazerat, the deputy for Dordogne, that
unless preventive steps were taken Hautefaye would become "the
center of a *jacquerie* that poses a serious threat to us in the region."
Our peasants, he added, "are Napoleonites or Jacquous."[86]

Anxiety appears to have run equally high in Nontron. On the
day after the murder the town organized its defenses against a
possible invasion by a "peasant horde" similar to the one that had
seized the town of Gourdon twenty-one years before. Rumors circulated of a plot to free prisoners from the town jail. The August
27 issue of *L'Echo de la Dordogne* reports that "town youths organized a civic guard and offered their assistance to the commandant
of the gendarmerie."

At a September hearing on a change in venue in the case, more
than five hundred people crowded the courtroom in Périgueux in
the hope of catching a glimpse of the "bloody horde."[87] When the
trial opened on December 13, the courtroom was full. Despite the
tragic war news, the chamber would remain full until the verdict
was announced on December 21. "The reserved seats in the semi-
circle behind the chief judge's chair were all occupied by ladies."[88]
Evariste Lestibeaudois, who supplied *L'Echo de la Dordogne* with
juicy eyewitness accounts of the proceedings, spoke of "opulent
bourgeois ladies who came to court as if to a theater." "Our theater,"
he added, "has been closed since the outbreak of hostilities."[89]
Conversations around the courtroom attested to the spectators'
"profound horror." People "pointed with disgust" at the prosecution exhibits, especially the two flat stones covered with the victim's
fat.[90] Alcide Dusolier would never forget the sight of them as they
lay in the office of the court clerk.[91]

Courtroom descriptions portrayed the monsters in their cage.

When the indictment was read, they listened "brutish and stony-faced." They gave the appearance of being "strangers to the dreadful crime" and remained "impassive."[92] In the latter stages of the trial, Ponsac described the accused as brutes who were as unfeeling as animals: "Chambort leaned on his elbows and held his head in his hands . . . Campot Junior, handkerchief in hand, rested his head on his left arm . . . Buisson let his head hang so that only his protruding nose was visible. Piarrouty looked like a dead man. His skin was livid, and his lifeless eyes stared at the ground. He appeared dazed and unfeeling. Mazière's eyes darted about like a badger's as he tried to hide himself in the midst of his codefendants. Only his eyes and pointy chin were visible."

On September 28, *L'Echo de la Dordogne* offered this explanation: "They all have the attitude, faces, and demeanor of poor, uncivilized peasants from the fringes of our *département*, along the border with Charente and Haute-Vienne." Here we see the beginnings of an interpretation in terms of primitiveness, of a resurgence of the primordial, of a geological rift that somehow allowed the prehistoric past to reemerge in that tragic year 1870. Yet we know full well that the peasants' crime would have seemed unremarkable only a few decades earlier.

Meanwhile, courtroom argument tended to blame the crime on mob psychology. From the outset, defense lawyers tried to prove that the murder was a collective act, that at least three hundred people had taken part, and that therefore their clients were simply scapegoats.[93] The accused attempted to shift the burden of responsibility to the group. Léonard Lamongie offered the opinion "that he had been urged on by the mob." Campot Senior admitted that he had been holding Monsieur de Monéys when he emerged from the sheepfold but insisted that he "did not hit him; it was the mob that beat him." Chambort, the ringleader, confessed: "I was mistaken. The frenzied mob . . . drove me wild and I lost my reason."[94]

In January 1871 the lawyers appealed to Adolphe Crémieux, the minister of justice, for a review of the case, which they described in these terms: "This was the crime of a mob in a moment of intoxication, fueled by ignorance, superstition, fanaticism, and the excitement of noise and numbers," all of which were "causes of frenzy."[95] Elsewhere they compare the event to an epidemic.

Historians who have looked at the crime of Hautefaye have also invoked mob psychology. Judge Simonet, in his 1929 Bordeaux lecture, referred to Taine, Tarde, and Le Bon and alluded to "improvised ringleaders" and to the credulity and suggestibility of "the collective soul."[96] The method is recognizable, as are its roots in the dominant social representations.

"The Populace of Peasants"

The Hautefaye tragedy confronted the republicans who took power on September 4 with a difficult problem. The affair inevitably became a topic of political debate, but it could not be accommodated neatly within existing political divisions and representations. The logic of the event was at variance with the logic of political analysis in the larger society.

Most republicans did not live in rural areas and had a poor understanding of rural society. According to Patrick Lacoste,[97] the leading republican militants active in Dordogne between 1870 and 1877 can be categorized as follows:

Members of liberal professions:	33.0% (134)	Small to medium bourgeoisie, essentially urban: 61.0%	71.5%
Industrialists and businessmen:	23.0% (93)		
Civil servants:	3.0% (13)		
White-collar workers:	2.0% (8)		
Blue-collar workers (almost all from Périgueux):	10.5% (40)		
Farmers, including wealthy landowners living in the city:	25.5% (102)		
Miscellaneous:	3.0%		

Note that here, as in Gard, some of these "farmers" probably threw their support to the government after the spring of 1871.[98]

In that terrible year, Dordogne republicans were well aware of the hatred that many of Périgord's peasants harbored toward them. Alcide Dusolier—who served briefly as subprefect of Nontron, was a friend of Gambetta's, and had once been a colleague of Alain de Monéys—detested what he called in his *Souvenirs* the "peasant riff-raff" (*populace de paysans*).[99] This "radical" (in the sense given to the word in 1869) thus borrowed the term conservatives used to express their contempt for the common people of the faubourgs and applied it to the peasants. In the eyes of this young lawyer and republican militant, peasants who banded together in mobs behaved like animals. In Hautefaye on the afternoon of August 16, the mob had been seized "by a kind of madness, similar to that which sometimes grips cattle forced to stand on sunbaked fairgrounds."[100]

Republican rancor toward the peasantry was clear in the aftermath of the plebiscite of May 8, 1870, and clearer still after the results of the February 8, 1871, National Assembly elections were announced. Jean Dubois, attentive to "emotional shifts" in the political and social vocabulary, has analyzed the rise of this negative attitude.[101] Republican contempt for rural folk can be traced back to 1863, when many inhabitants of the countryside voted for the imperial candidates. The process began to intensify in 1869, when the words "peasant" and "rural" took on markedly pejorative overtones. The elections of February 1871 gave concrete meaning to these negative connotations, meaning that was summed up in the expressions "rural majority" and "Assembly of hicks." Jean Faury notes that this hostility toward rural people was expressed openly in nearby Tarn. On February 12, 1871, *La Patriote,* a paper published in that *département,* observed: "The peasant, more often nasty than stupid, is generally a thief if he is a tenant, a usurer if he is a landlord, and a coward unless he has been transformed by a stint in the military or time in the city. [And since most peasants will be ruined by Prussia's exactions], we say, even at the risk of being accused of cruelty, that we shall, with the utmost pleasure, refuse bread to any peasant whom hunger may bring to our door and shall applaud with joy if he should be deprived of his sons. Let the wretched brute who places the emperor above the people and animals before family go find what he needs in Berlin."[102]

Dordogne was no less harsh in its judgment. Albert Theulier, the subprefect of Ribérac, wrote Alcide Dusolier on December 31, 1870: "As for the peasants, their spirit is detestable . . . The government must rely firmly on the armed cities, which thank God are not about to allow their intellectual and moral existence to be overrun by those wretched hayseeds. Until they've been educated (which won't be any time soon), there is only one argument against them: brute force. They respect only one man, the gendarme, and I certainly hope that you will not commit the extraordinary error of pardoning the miserable murderers of Hautefaye."[103] On this score he offers a piece of advice: "No tears for four wild animals of that sort. Leave the humanitarian sniveling for better days. Shoot the traitors and guillotine the murderers. This is where six months of war have led a former opponent of the death penalty."

Yet the Hautefaye affair did prove embarrassing for certain republicans. The peasants on the fairground had directed their wrath at nobles and curés. They had risen up against those who, in their eyes, were dealing with the enemy. Their attitude was in some ways similar to that of the "Blues," the heroes of 1792, staunch defenders of France and, withing limits, of the Revolution.

Thus the republicans' response to the problems raised by the tragedy of August 16 was not without ambiguity. Their first thought was to wipe out every trace of the crime. They considered striking the name of the murderous commune from the map, a move advocated in early September by Dusolier, then subprefect. On September 23 *L'Echo de la Dordogne* offered the opinion that such a decision would be popular. On that day Dr. Guilbert, a Freemason and psychiatrist who had been named prefect of the *département* on September 5, conveyed the Nontron district's wishes to the ministry of the interior.[104]

The administration, however, soon abandoned the proposal. On September 22 the innkeeper Elie Mondout, serving as temporary mayor of Hautefaye, argued skillfully in defense of the commune, and he was followed on October 9 by young Villard, the law student who had been born in Hautefaye.[105] French law recognized only individual criminal responsibility. Camille de Maillard and Alain de Monéys had undeniably been irresponsible in uttering "imprudent words" in tragic wartime circumstances. Hautefaye clearly stood firm. The residents certainly would not accept responsibility for the tragedy. There had been four or five hundred madmen in the mob according to the mayor and seven or eight hundred according to Villard, but only forty to fifty people lived in Hautefaye and some of them had attempted to stop the attackers. Only three residents, one of them a child, had been involved in the assault. Elie Mondout protested, not without reason, that Hautefaye, "the most tranquil village in France," had been transformed in the public mind into a "den of thieves." The commune had "suffered an indelible stain." For this the government was clearly responsible: the imperial authorities had failed to organize the national guard, no gendarmes were present on the fairground on the afternoon of the tragedy, and, worst of all, the few "Messieurs" present that day had chosen to flee or to watch from the sidelines. Must "Hautefaye be sacrificed because it is short of influential figures?"

The new subprefect proved susceptible to all these arguments. On October 27 he advised Dr. Guilbert to demonstrate leniency toward a commune that was at worst guilty of "weakness," "indifference," and "abstention."[106] Furthermore, breaking up the commune would give rise to lasting hatreds between "the annexed residents and those who stood to gain by their annexation," and such hatreds, young Villard argued, "are a fateful heritage transmitted from generation to generation." In other words, Alcide Dusolier and Dr. Guilbert had failed to appreciate the difficulties involved in abolishing a village community.

The subprefect therefore toyed with another idea: to try expiation, as governments had done during the Restoration. "I would favor requiring the commune to build an expiatory cross or column [note the hesitation] and urge that it be punished, along with neighboring communes, by closing down the Hautefaye fairs." The writer has clearly grasped the fact that the murder involved people not just from the commune itself but from the whole area served by the fair. The authorities, however, rejected his pious advice.

The republicans turned out to be more interested in using the tragedy than in organizing expiatory ceremonies. The torture of Alain de Monéys proved a boon for those who wished to reshape political imagery. In order for republicans to profit from the event, blame for the barbarous crime had to be placed squarely on the tottering empire. Horror and dread were enlisted in the service of politics. The Second Empire, republicans argued, had no right to portray itself as the enemy and vanquisher of peasant violence in December 1851, the proof being that in 1870 it was the cause of such violence. The barbaric, primitive, and blind rage of August 16, 1870, stemmed directly from the coup d'état of December 2, 1851. The Hautefaye crime linked the beginning and the end of Napoleon III's "Caesarean" regime. The true significance of the bloodless revolution of September 4 stood out with shining clarity when compared with the "Bonapartist *jacquerie*" of August 16.[107]

The Hautefaye crime, Charles Ponsac wrote in February 1871,

was a result of the "brutality injected [into the region] by the Empire."[108] "By burning a man in the emperor's name, these peasants condemned the fallen regime more thoroughly than even the poet of *Les châtiments* [Victor Hugo]." "It took imperial means to inculcate such wild hopes—hopes of reward—into human skulls, especially the thick skulls of brutes." Thus, there was a subtle link between the imperial feast and the barbarity of Hautefaye.

"It was to shouts of 'Vive Napoléon!' that this mad multitude danced around the young martyr," Dusolier wrote in 1874.[109] "Yes, for our rural areas, the emperor was like a God." The blame for the incineration of Alain de Monéys should be attributed, Dusolier argued, to "Bonapartist myths," which urged peasants to avenge themselves against nobles, curés, and republicans. The young republican forgot that for three years he and his friends had been more active than the imperial government in raising the specter of reinstitution of seigneurial dues and the tithe.[110] What concerns us here, however, is only the way in which this propaganda affected representations.

The Empire was also to blame for the ignorance of the peasantry: "O! Cursed be the ignorance that permits such savagery in 1871 *[sic]*. Through his vote the peasant will kill our freedom as surely as he killed Monsieur de Monéys."[111] In other words, the behavior of the Hautefaye mob proved that peasants remained brutes, and that is why they did not vote republican. They did vote for the Empire, thereby proving that they were primitive, barbaric, and irrational. Social representations and political representations were inextricably intertwined. The same reasoning that explained the peasants' rage also justified their enemies' hatred. Republican logic and conservative political rationality functioned in similar ways. In both, ethical judgment played a primary role: the political enemy was portrayed as wicked and backward. "Urban rabble" and "rural riff-raff" formed mirror images.

Thus, it was with a clear conscience that the republican government refused to show leniency toward the accused. Hautefaye's dread savages were "Bonapartist" barbarians who thought they were roasting a republican—that is, a progressive. This attitude seems to have troubled some officials, however, particularly Dr. Guilbert. If the crime was indeed a political crime, then was not the Republic simply repeating the sins of the previous regime by punishing it so harshly? Was there not a danger that the Parisian spirit of September 4 would be contradicted by the severity of the court in Périgueux?

Some people wanted to interpret the event in political terms, others to treat it as a common felony. The minister of justice quickly decided to exclude the murderers of Hautefaye from the amnesty granted on September 4 to all who had been found guilty of political offenses since December 2, 1851. Yet the defense attorneys, all of whom were republicans, continued to the very end to cling to the hope that the crime would ultimately be classified as political. In their eyes, "political passion" was the sole motive for the murder.[112] They used the pejorative vocabulary of the Second Empire to save their clients. Loyalty to the fallen regime could only lead to moral disarray. The murderers' sole crime, therefore, was credulity. But the minister of justice stood by his September 14 directive: "Murderers guilty of having burned a man alive cannot be included in the amnesty simply because they made their unfortunate victim shout 'Vive l'Empereur!'"[113]

The minister's argument was a powerful one, but his contention that the rioters burned their victim alive would be challenged during the trial. His statement also ran counter to a republican tradition of leniency toward murderous mobs. At the outbreak of revolution in Paris in February 1848, democrats in Limoges had headed straight for the prison to demand the release of the murderers—or at any rate the least compromised among those accused of the murder—of young Chambert. A decree of February 29, 1848, had nullified all "sentences handed down for political acts" and "canceled current prosecutions."[114] And there is no evidence, so far as I am aware, that the murderers of gendarmes in Bédarieux and Clamecy (1851) had been excluded from the amnesty. Be that as it may, the Hautefaye defense attorneys' request for appeal was rejected on January 30, 1871. Justice minister Crémieux "ordered immediate execution of the death sentence" against the accused.[115] The executions were set for February 6.

The prefect of Dordogne, well aware of the political nature and implications of the crime, professed dismay at the sentence. February 4 and 5 were distressing days for him. On the fourth he sent two dispatches to Bordeaux, where a part of the government of national defense had established its headquarters.[116] At 7:40 p.m. he asked if there "might not be a stay of execution in Hautefaye. Does this mean there will be no pardon?" At 10:20 his tone was more urgent: "The execution at Hautefaye must be stayed, for given the fact that voting is to take place on February 8, it could be seen at this time as a political execution." On February 5 he was insistent: "It seems to me urgent that the four executions in Hautefaye be stayed. They may well have the most deplorable consequences. Or, if they cannot be stayed, pardon must be granted . . . Immediate response."

The response was indeed immediate—and merciless: in the absence of Crémieux, who had left for Paris, Gambetta, to whom all the dispatches had been routed, decided that there would be no stay.

The Guillotine in the Field

The "monsters" were stunned by the news. The imperial government had categorically disavowed those who had believed they were acting in its behalf. On August 19, 1870, the *procureur général* of the Bordeaux court spoke in a letter to the minister of "frightful scenes" in Dordogne.[117] The next day the *Moniteur* inveighed against the "horrors." The authorities reacted quickly. The chief participants in the drama were arrested on the night of August 16. On August 24 the pusillanimous mayor, Mathieu, was removed from office by governmental decree. Elie Mondout was named acting mayor. *L'Echo de la Dordogne* published word of these changes in its August 27 issue, and the subprefect of Nontron publicly stripped the unfortunate blacksmith of his mayoral sash.[118]

The disarray of the local peasants in the face of these developments is not hard to imagine. Trusting in the imperial government, convinced that the rumors of treasonous activity by nobles, curés, and republicans were true, and certain that they had acted in "their" emperor's behalf and deserved a reward, they found themselves castigated by representatives of the empress Eugénie, regent for her husband, who was at the front. Their consternation was understandably as great as their former devotion.

The fall of the Empire only compounded their disappointment. The government's refusal to grant amnesty had marked a departure from its policy of leniency toward rural troublemakers. In court the accused peasants had to face the withering irony of their judges, who mocked their political beliefs. During the December trial, for example, Mazière was accused of having said, "We killed him to save France. Our emperor will save us in return." The trial minutes record what happened next: "The prosecutor made an ironic gesture and sat down, saying, 'Then go find your emperor now.' (Laughter in the courtroom.)"[119]

On December 21 sentence was passed, and it was unusually harsh: Chambort, Buisson, Piarrouty, and Mazière were sentenced to death, and the younger Campot to life at hard labor. Eight others received sentences of five to eight years at hard labor; the elderly Sallat got five years in prison. Five other peasants received prison terms. Young Thibaud Limay was sent to a house of correction. In all, nineteen individuals were severely punished for the murder of Alain de Monéys. The republican courts proved no less harsh than those of the July Monarchy.[120] In 1847 the jury of notables that had met in Bourges to judge those accused of murdering young Chambert had issued three death sentences, nineteen terms at hard labor, and one term in a penitentiary.[121]

When the verdict was read, the accused seemed at first dazed, then terrified. Only Léonard Piarrouty gave in to anger and launched a salvo of insults at his judges. One witness, Evariste Lestibeaudois, reported that "a chorus of protest rose from the common people in the audience . . . The crowd remained in front of the courthouse for a long time and refused to disperse, despite the cold and drizzle."[122]

The series of disappointments did not end there, however. A month later the peasants of the Nontron district learned that requests for pardon and stay of execution had been denied. The short time between sentencing and execution was striking, as was the government's determination to cast Hautefaye as the center of a "Bonapartist *jacquerie*." No expiatory column was erected. Instead, the guillotine, in a scene worthy of Victor Hugo's *Quatre-vingt-treize*, would mark the spot with a pool of blood. Previous executions in the region had been conducted in Périgueux, but this time the *bois de justice*, the wooden structure of the guillotine, was transported to the scene of the crime.[123] This was not actually a new idea. In 1815 the government of the Second Restoration had moved a guillotine from village to village to mete out punishment for disturbances in the Grenoble area. And on April 16, 1847, a shoemaker named Michot, aged twenty-five, and his two companions were beheaded on the village square in Buzançais. Thus, the government of national defense based its decision on a well-established tradition.

In Hautefaye and the surrounding countryside, however, the execution, as even the prefect conceded, was considered to be an act of political retribution. For this reason, moving the guillotine through the *département* was not without problems. On February 5 at around five in the afternoon, the four condemned men confessed and received communion.[124] At eight o'clock they were handed over to the executioner. Accompanied by two clergymen, he took his seat in the carriage that was to transport the condemned men to the place of execution. The journey took place at night. Flanked by mounted gendarmes, the somber convoy slowly covered the thirty-five miles between Périgueux and the hamlet of Hautefaye. By midnight it had reached Brantôme, where a second team of horses replaced the first. At three in the morning there was a second change of horses in Mareuil, and at five the convoy reached its destination. The condemned men were placed in the home of Antony, some forty yards from the marketplace, where work began on the scaffold.[125] Lack of room to work made the job difficult.

The account of the four men's final moments conforms to the edifying tradition of such tales and is not to be relied on.[126] The scene is reminiscent of the vigil on the place de Grève in Paris, and the old ceremony of confession.[127] Piarrouty was the only one of the four men to ask for soup and a glass of spirits, about whose quality he complained. He then began a remorseful lament: "Parents," he maintained, "are almost always the cause of their children's woes. They don't raise them Christianly." To the boy who served him coffee he said, "Little one, be good. Don't follow our example." Chambort, meanwhile, cried and seemed genuinely repentant. Mazière, "sobbing, uttered several times the name of his poor mother, who he said would die of anguish." Recall that all four men had been upstanding citizens prior to the sad events of August 16. As the end neared they asked that their families be urged to pay certain recently acquired debts. The only dark spot in this otherwise edifying picture was the anger of Léonard Piarrouty: the redoubtable ragpicker of Nontronneau roundly castigated the executioner's assistant, who he said was ripping his fine clothes for no good reason.

The execution took place between 8:25 and 8:30 in the morning before a detachment of two hundred infantrymen who had set up camp in Hautefaye the previous night, reinforced by the gendarmes who had escorted the guillotine. No wonder the peasants of the Nontron district saw this show of force as a political statement: no troops had been stationed in the village since the fall of the previous republic.

Abandoned by the rest of society, the rural people of the Hautefaye region felt totally isolated. Their emotions were a mixture of confusion, helplessness, and rancor. There were plenty of signs that peasants remained firm in their political loyalties, as the sub-prefect of Ribérac fearfully noted. Antirepublican rumors had been circulating since August. In late September the prefect, Guilbert, sent a memorandum to the mayors of his *département*: "Unfortunate rumors have been circulating: that the Republic is not in firm control, that the former emperor is about to return, that his son is already in Paris, and so on."[128] He urged mayors to report anyone spreading seditious rumors, so that they could be arrested and placed on trial.

On December 31 Albert Theulier, the subprefect of Ribérac (outside the Nontron district), spoke in a letter of "the angry reaction in the countryside."[129] The peasants' state of mind was "deplorable." There were rumors that "the republicans are lining their pockets with [the peasants'] money. Official dispatches [are regarded] as so many lies . . . The most incredible statements are made publicly." Once again the alleged circulation of money was the focal point of many rumors, and the peasants of Périgord looked upon republicans as looters of the public coffers.

During the night preceding the execution, two innkeepers in Mareuil reportedly refused to serve the executioners. Only a handful of spectators turned out to see the four men die. "If there were a hundred I would be surprised," wrote Charles Ponsac.[130] This was decidedly a small crowd compared with the huge throngs that turned out to watch other nineteenth-century executions.

Chambort, Buisson, Mazière, and Piarrouty were perceived as martyrs, to the dismay of the curé of Saint-Pardoux, a small parish near Nontron: "The peasant's moral sense is so perverted," he wrote to his bishop, "that he regards the men executed at Hautefaye as martyrs. No one can deny this with impunity."[131] The peasants of the region annoyed nobles, curés, and republicans by flocking to the Hautefaye fairs, which the government had considered shutting down and which nobles had forbidden their tenants to attend. Members of the clerical party and militant republicans in the region continued to voice hostility to the violent peasantry as they had done under the imperial regime, but now the peasants laughed at their threats. On May 7, 1872, Monsieur de Lasfond described the situation in a letter: "All of us have forbidden our tenants to take their livestock to the fair in Hautefaye, where we shall never again set foot." But "the tenants pride themselves on going there, saying [in dialect], 'The gentlemen won't go, but we will.' So in fact there are more fairs now than in the past, and for the 'Jacques' they are a focal point of covert agitation and hatred."[132] He added that the commune of Beaussac had expressed a wish to meet in Hautefaye. For Lasfond, this wish (which so far as I know is not confirmed by any archival document) was an expression of approval of the murder of Alain de Monéys and a way for the commune to thumb its nose at the aristocracy.

The transport of the guillotines to Hautefaye left profound traces in memory. In 1970 Jean-Louis Galet met a woman from Mareuil who confided to him that "my great-aunt told me the story many times."[133] But in the presence of strangers those old people who knew of the event took refuge in silence. The Hautefaye affair and the sentiments it aroused became part of the secret lore of the local peasantry, along with other never-to-be-divulged scandals, misdeeds, and tragedies.

Philippe Joutard has observed that bloodshed is a necessary condition for the constitution of indelible memories.[134] His argument appears to be corroborated by the results of our microhistorical analysis. A tragic mythology grew out of the event. It was alleged that Anne Mondout died three days after the execution because the horrible spectacle was too much for her to bear. Thus, at least one resident of the "village of cannibals" possessed as delicate a sensibility as anyone could wish. Many popular movements have in fact adopted a tragic young woman or virgin as their symbol.[135]

The National Assembly elections that were held two days after the executions confirmed that political sentiments in the region had not changed. The magnitude of the republican defeat in the Hautefaye area would be astonishing if one knew nothing of the trauma that people had just been through. In the canton of Champagnac-de-Belair the self-styled "liberal" list received 82 percent of the votes, compared with 4 percent for the republicans. In the canton of Bussière-Badil, the corresponding figures were 93 percent and 6 percent. In the canton of Nontron, where votes from the town were counted along with those from small rural communes such as Hautefaye, the results were 78 percent and 18 percent.

Alcide Dusolier, who had been subprefect of the district in September 1870, presented himself to voters as "Gambetta's secretary." In the three cantons mentioned above, he received 6 percent, 6 percent, and 20 percent of the vote respectively. In the canton of Champagnac-de-Belair he lost by a large margin to none other than Napoleon III and by an even larger margin to the imperial prince. In the canton of Mareuil "the emperor" defeated all the republican candidates except Dusolier and the former deputy Delbetz. He received more than four times as many votes as Louis Mie. And bear in mind that neither the deposed sovereign nor his son figured on any list of candidates.[136]

I agree with Stéphane Audoin-Rouzeau that the political significance of the February 8 election is often underestimated.[137] Historians traditionally have emphasized the abnormal conditions in which this election was held. Many voters were still held prisoner or in transit. The campaign was too brief to be more than a travesty. In the wake of Jules Simon's abrogation of Gambetta's decree, Bonapartists either did not dare to run or believed that they would be prohibited from filing as candidates. None of these matters is in doubt. Furthermore, the election was in a sense seen as a referendum: voters were asked to declare themselves either for or against a resumption of hostilities. Yet these arguments often conceal a disingenuous refusal to accept the fact that the republicans did not do very well in the February voting. In February 1871 republican voters remained—much as they had been in May 1870—largely in the minority outside the major cities. This assertion is often challenged, but the objections raised have remarkably little substance. Republican gains in the summer by-elections of 1871 prove nothing, for instance, because the massacre of the Paris Commune in May ensured that the emotional climate and, even more important, the way people saw the political situation were dramatically different in July from what they had been in February.

Another often repeated argument is that, in the February 8 elections, peasants, like so much dead weight, simply reverted to their old habits of subservience; owing to the collapse of the imperial government, we are told, they once again came under the sway of traditional notables. It is never suggested that this choice might have been the result not of mere inertia but of an analysis of the political situation. But let us consider the peasants of the Nontron district and try to ascertain the logic of their behavior. Once again the Republic had deceived and crushed a group that had only recently demonstrated fervent loyalty to the emperor. It was easy for the peasants to conclude that the most effective and implacable of "their" sovereign's enemies, and those responsible for his downfall, were the republicans. Furthermore, in a rural society undermined by the decline of its bourgeoisie, aristocrats and peasants were joined in a kind of regional solidarity, particularly after hostility to the nobility declined as rumors of aristocratic support for Prussia became irrelevant and concerns about reinstatement of the tithe and seigneurial dues faded. In short, there was a logic in the peasants' refusal to vote republican that had nothing to do with unwillingness to continue the war.

The subsequent evolution of peasant attitudes in Dordogne is beyond the scope of this book. I would simply point out that, as Ralph Gibson notes, when the time came to take a position on the new regime, the people of rural Périgord remained hostile to the anonymous and oligarchic Republic of the Opportunists. A majority of peasants did come to support the Republic, but they voted for those candidates who held out the prospect of a different type of regime: the Republic of the Radicals and, briefly, of the Boulangists.[138] But it is not my task here to analyze the transformation of "Napoleonic" or "imperialist" peasants into supporters of the Radical party.[139]

Conclusion

The torture and murder at Hautefaye was, and proclaimed itself to be, a political act. Personal revenge, so far as we can tell, played no part in the crime. Its motives were not those of the usual violent crime. The murder had a coherence and logic of its own. The peasants involved did not behave irrationally; they did, however, interpret the political situation in terms of their own independent system of representations.

The significance of the crime was covered up. The peasants' act was disapproved by the rest of society, disavowed by the Empire, and treated as a common crime by the Republic because after nineteen years of universal suffrage, murder and mayhem had ceased to be acceptable forms of political expression.[1] A Dionysiac outburst had ended in horror. To people imbued with the new sensibility, the assailants' actions immediately suggested atavistic forms of violence and cannibalism. The crime gave new currency to the cliché "monster."

The blood shed by the guillotine was not enough to compensate for the cruelty at Hautefaye. True, in a small number of rural communities, Léonard Piarrouty and his friends were seen as martyrs. But the logic of their behavior was buried and forgotten along with Buisson's bloody stake. Demoted to the status of a common crime, their act of torture was drained of its meaning; its strangeness was limited to its atavistic character. Historians ceased to be interested in the murder when they found that it could not be explained in terms of the same political divisions they used to make sense of the larger society. This cavalier neglect is a sign of the true importance of the case. The reaction to the burning of Alain de Monéys is a striking indication of how rapidly the average nineteenth-century person had lost touch with the everyday violence of another era. It throws into sharp relief an anthropological transformation that had been under way since the first emergence of *l'âme sensible,* the sensitive soul.

Historians' avoidance of the issue is an obstacle in the path of anyone who wishes to measure the consternation, solitude, and anguish of the Nontronnais villagers, whose only means of dealing with their total isolation after August 1870 was to respond with scornful silence and smoldering hostility. Before being disavowed by the society that surrounded them, these peasants had found no way to express their unique conception of politics, their deep suffering, and their fierce loyalty to the emperor other than to torture their enemy. The emotions of the day having ebbed, nothing remains of this forgotten and inarticulate assertion of identity but the naked cruelty of the act.

Notes

The Incident

1. Charles Ponsac, *Le crime d'Hautefaye* (Bordeaux: Viéville et Capiomont, 1871), foreword.

1. A Consistency of Sentiment

1. In this connection, compare Carlo Ginzburg's notion of an indicative paradigm.
2. Ralph Gibson, "Les notables et l'Eglise dans le diocèse de Périgueux" (diss., University of Lyons III, 1979), vol. 1, p. 64.
3. At the height of the Second Empire, Audiganne overestimated the extent of sharecropping in Périgord. See his "Le métayage et la culture dans le Périgord: Voyage au château de Montaigne," *Revue des deux mondes* 19, no. 3 (1867): 613–645.
4. In analyzing social practices, however, it is difficult to distinguish clearly between what is reality and what is fantasy.
5. Gibson, "Les notables," vol. 2, p. 446.
6. For a magnificent account of the origins of antinoble sentiment, see Antoine de Baecque, "Le discours anti-noble (1787–1792): Aux origines d'un slogan—Le peuple contre les gros," *Revue d'histoire moderne et contemporaine* 36 (January–March 1989): 3–28.
7. Prefect of Dordogne to minister of the interior, 4 February 1852, *Archives Nationales* F1 c III Dordogne 7.
8. The Nontron district was a region devoted to the raising of livestock, as Gibson points out ("Les notables," vol. 1, p. 152), and it main-

tained its population longer than did the regions of diversified farming in the Dordogne valley.

9. For a detailed analysis, see Gibson, "Les notables," vol. 1, pp. 126ff.

10. In the Nontron district in the period 1839–1841, 47.7 percent of the voters paid less than three hundred francs in taxes and 77.8 percent paid less than five hundred francs. See Gibson, "Les notables," vol. 1, p. 74.

11. Ibid., vol. 2, p. 448. Certain nobles, such as Bugeaud and the marquis de Fayolle, took a lively interest in agronomy, but they were exceptions to the rule.

12. Ibid.

13. To the dismay of the anxious Maine de Biran, who complains constantly about this in his *Journal*.

14. Data in Gibson, "Les notables," vol. 1, p. 246. For comparisons with thirteen other regions, see Maurice Agulhon, Louis Girard, et al., *Les maires en France du Consulat à nos jours* (Paris: Publications de la Sorbonne, 1986).

15. One sign: in the 1830 elections, four enemies of the Polignac ministry and only two supporters (who subsequently took an oath of allegiance to Louis-Philippe) were elected to the Chamber of Deputies. The Périgord deputies proved to be more "ministerial" under the July Monarchy than under the previous regime. See Gibson, "Les notables," vol. 1, pp. 23–24.

16. Ibid., vol. 1, p. 255.

17. The government used similar tactics in eastern Aquitaine. See André Armengaud, *Les populations de l'Est-aquitaine au début de l'époque contemporaine* (Paris and The Hague: Mouton, 1961).

18. Gibson, "Les notables," vol. 2, p. 446.

19. *Archives Diocésaines* D 9, cited in Gibson, "Les notables," vol. 1, p. 257.

20. See Michel Denis, *Les royalistes de la Mayenne et le monde moderne* (Paris: Klincksieck, 1977).

21. On the influence of irony on political practice in rural central France, see Yves Pourcher, "La politique au risque de la moquerie," in *La moquerie: Dires et pratiques—Le monde Alpin et Rhodanien* 3–4 (1988): 191–207, esp. p. 198, on the role of laughter in "building the boundaries of political allegiance."

22. Aside from an interesting special issue of the journal *Le genre humain* (no. 5, 1982) devoted to this topic, and aside from Michel-Louis Rouquette, *Les rumeurs* (Paris: Presses Universitaires de France, 1975). Bronislaw Baczko deplores the way in which historians of the French Revolution disdain the importance of rumor; see his *Comment*

sortir de la Terreur: Thermidor et la Révolution (Paris: Gallimard, 1989), p. 17.

23. Lydia Flem, "Bouche bavarde et oreille curieuse," *Le genre humain* 5 (1982), special issue entitled *La rumeur* (Paris: Fayard, 1982), p. 18.

24. Ibid.

25. Supplanting an earlier form of solidarity explored by Yves-Marie Bercé, *Histoire des Croquants: Etude des soulèvements populaires au XVIIe siècle dans le Sud-Ouest de la France* (Geneva and Paris: Droz, 1974), pp. 127–129. In the seventeenth century, nobles offered refuge to peasants pursued by agents of the salt tax and protected them against thieves, undue billeting of soldiers, and other exigencies of the state.

26. The expression is used by Pierre Lévêque, "La Révolution de 1815: Le mouvement populaire pendant les Cent Jours," in *Les Cent Jours dans l'Yonne: Aux origines du bonapartisme libéral* (Paris: Maison des Sciences de l'Homme, 1988). See also the classic by Henry Houssaye, *1815* (Paris: Perrin, 1893), vol. 1: *La première Restauration: Le retour de l'Ile de l'Elbe, les Cent Jours,* which provides indications of violent demonstrations of hostility to the nobility. On the whole period 1814–1815, the best work is still Félix Ponteil, *La chute de Napoléon Ier et la crise française de 1814–1815* (Paris: Aubier, 1943).

27. By this he meant that the composition of the nobility was not the same for the rural populace as it was for the enlightened segment of the population to which he belonged. He implies that peasants included "rich" commoners in what they called the nobility.

28. *Arch. Nat.* BB30 374, emphasis added.

29. This similarity did not escape the notice of Stéphane Audoin-Rouzeau, who discusses the Hautefaye tragedy in *1870: La France dans la guerre* (Paris: Armand Colin, 1989), p. 130.

30. Quoted in Georges Rocal, "La Révolution de 1830 en Dordogne," *Bulletin de la Société Historique et Archéologique du Périgord* (1936), p. 271. To set these regional disturbances in their national context, see Pamela Pilbeam, "Popular Violence in Provincial France after the 1830 Revolution," *English Historical Review* 91, no. 359 (1976): 278–297; and idem, "The Three Glorious Days: The Revolution of 1830 in Provincial France," *Historical Journal* 26, no. 4 (1983): 831–844. See also John Merriman, ed., *1830 in France* (New York and London, 1975), and the old but detailed article by Roger Price, "Popular Disturbances in the French Provinces after the July Revolution of 1830," *European Studies Review* 1, no. 4 (1971): 323–350. Price looks at the hostility of peasants in Corrèze toward

nobles, the rich, and members of the clergy (p. 344). There were attacks on châteaux in the *département* in the aftermath of the July Revolution. In Chamberet the situation was similar to that in Pazayac. Price's excellent essay thus corroborates my findings— namely, that social antagonism in the region took certain characteristic forms and that implicit references to the Revolution were commonplace.

31. *Arch. Nat.* F7 9471, previously used by Rocal, "La Révolution de 1830 en Dordogne," pp. 399–403.

32. On this violence, see Alain Corbin, *Archaïsme et modernité en Limousin au XIXe siècle, 1845–1880* (Paris: Marcel Rivière, 1975), vol. 1, pp. 500–502.

33. Georges Rocal, *1848 en Dordogne* (Paris: Occitania, 1934), vol. 1, p. 27, and, for the attack on La Durantie, pp. 105ff.

34. Gibson, "Les notables," pp. 254–255.

35. Rocal, *1848 en Dordogne*, vol. 1, pp. 142–143.

36. *Arch. Nat.* BB18 1254, emphasis added.

37. *Procureur général*, 18 July 1849, *Arch. Nat.* BB30, 359.

38. For this and subsequent quotes, see Rocal, *1848 en Dordogne*, vol. 2, pp. 102–106 and 247.

39. Gibson, "Les notables," vol. 1, p. 258.

40. I use the word "curé" rather than "priest" or "clergyman" in order to reflect as accurately as possible the vocabulary used by rural people themselves.

41. In the Nontron district between 1836 and 1844 only eight of fifty-four vestry council chairmen were nobles. Gibson, "Les notables," vol. 1, p. 332, and, for subsequent details, pp. 266–287.

42. Along with nine individuals of dubious nobility. Gibson, "Les notables," vol. 2, p. 385. The situation was very different from that which Yves Pourcher found in the Lozère in *Les maîtres de granit: Les notables de Lozère, du XVIIIe siècle à nos jours* (Paris: Orban, 1987), passim.

43. Only 24 percent of the curés in the Périgueux district reported such a situation.

44. Gibson, "Les notables," vol. 2, p. 550.

45. See especially Maurice Agulhon, *La République au village* (Paris: Plon, 1970), pp. 172–188; and, for a nearby region, Corbin, *Archaïsme et modernité*, vol. 1, pp. 647–652.

46. Note of the Ministry of the Interior, May 1865, *Arch. Nat.* F1 cIII Dordogne 11.

47. More precisely, the portion of the choir around the altar. On the burning of church pews and revolutionary symbolism in the peasant

tradition, particularly in Périgord, see Mona Ozouf, *La fête révolutionnaire, 1789–1799* (Paris: Gallimard, 1976), pp. 388–440.

48. *Procureur général* of Bordeaux to the minister of justice, 11 June and 7 September 1838, *Arch. Nat.* BB18 1254.

49. *Procureur du roi* for Dordogne to the minister of justice, 28 June 1838, *Arch. Nat.* BB18 1254.

50. *Procureur du roi*, Nontron, to the minister of justice, 2 July 1838, *Arch. Nat.* BB18 1254.

51. Court of Nontron, 5 July 1838, *Arch. Nat.* BB18 1254.

52. *Procureur* of Nontron to *procureur général*, 17 July 1838, ibid.

53. *Procureur* of Dordogne, 28 June 1838, ibid.

54. Note from the Direction de la Police Générale, 2 August 1838, ibid.

55. Mayor of Sourzac, *Archives Départementales de la Dordogne* 1 M 72.

56. This and the following quotations are from Rocal, *1848 en Dordogne*, vol. 2, p. 247. On the outcome of this affair, see *Arch. Nat.* BB30 359.

57. *Arch. Nat.* F1 c III Dordogne 11.

58. Letter from prefect to minister of the interior, 1 April 1870, ibid.

59. Note from minister of the interior concerning the fires in Dordogne, 4 September 1862, *Arch. Nat.* F1 c III Dordogne 11.

60. Report of the *procureur impérial*, 28 August 1862, ibid. The two subsequent quotes are from the same source. This affair seems to have involved a resurgence of the fear of aristocratic arsonists that broke out in Burgundy in 1846. See Eugen Weber, *Peasants into Frenchmen* (Stanford: Stanford University Press, 1976).

61. This affair is described in Jean Maurain, *La politique ecclésiastique du Second Empire de 1852 à 1869* (Paris: Alcan, 1930), and in Weber, *Peasants*. Yves-Marie Bercé has examined it in greater detail in *Croquants et nu-pieds: Les soulèvements paysans en France du XVIe au XIXe siècle* (Paris: Gallimard, 1974), pp. 214–221. Baron Eschassériaux discusses it at length in his *Mémoires*; see François Pairault, "Les mémoires d'un grand notable bonapartiste: Le baron Eschassériaux de Saintes, 1823–1906" (diss., University of Paris X–Nanterre, 1990), pp. 96–98.

62. Report on application for pardon, 5 October 1868, *Arch. Nat.* BB24 721; subsequent quotes are from the same source. According to Eugen Weber, the troubles began when the Lestranges decided to have their coat of arms inscribed on the windows of the church of Chevanceaux.

63. Ibid.

64. Ibid.

65. Memoirs of Baron Eschassériaux, in Pairault, "Les Mémoires," p. 97.

66. On the Donnezac disturbances, see *Arch. Nat.* BB24 721.
67. *Procureur général* of Poitiers to minister of justice, *Arch. Nat.* BB24 721.
68. On the Sigogne disturbances, see *Arch. Nat.* BB24 721.
69. See Jean Faury, *Cléricalisme et anticléricalisme dans le Tarn, 1848–1900* (Toulouse: Presses de l'Université de Toulouse–Le Mirail, 1980). In February 1869, for example, after a drawing of lots for military service, conscripts from Périgueux staged a noisy demonstration against the bishop. Report from prefect to minister of the interior, 10 February 1869, *Arch. Nat.* F1 c III Dordogne 7.
70. In *Arch. Nat.* F1 c III Dordogne 11.
71. Prefect to minister of interior, 12 July 1869, *Arch. Nat.* F1 c III Dordogne 7.
72. A very revealing text on this subject can be found in Armengaud, *Les populations de l'Est-aquitaine,* pp. 480–482.
73. Rocal, "La Révolution de 1830."
74. See the theoretical reflections of Peter McPhee, "La mainmorte du passé? Les images de la Révolution française dans les mobilisations politiques rurales sous la Seconde République," in Michel Vovelle, ed., *L'image de la Révolution française* (Paris: Pergamon, 1989), vol. 2, pp. 1556–1562.
75. See the classic account by Georges Lefebvre, *La Grande Peur de 1789* (Paris: Armand Colin, 1988), with Jacques Revel's new introduction. The commune of Ruffec was the epicenter of the phenomenon. Mona Ozouf has studied manifestations of the Fear in nearby Lot. Disturbances erupted here at the end of 1789 and throughout 1790. Mobs set fire to church pews and tore down weathercocks and other symbols of prominence. Ozouf identifies a liberal discourse and a repressive discourse in the representation of the events. See Mona Ozouf, "Entre la fête et l'émeute: L'hiver 1790 en Quercy," in *Révolution et traditions en vicomté de Turenne . . . 1738–1889* (Saint-Céré, 1989), pp. 165–174.
76. *Archives Diocésaines* C 7. Parish monographs (Villars), cited in Gibson, "Les notables," vol. 1, p. 20.
77. As well as forms of violence against nobles and curés.
78. Note the time difference.
79. Rocal, *1848 en Dordogne,* vol. 1, p. 141.
80. Ibid., p. 142.
81. On that day a demonstration by socialist-democrats turned into an insurrection, which ended in failure only after the insurgents had taken up positions in the Conservatoire des Arts et Métiers. Ledru-Rollin was obliged to flee in the aftermath of these events.

82. See *Arch. Dép. Dordogne* 1 M. 72. Report of the subprefect of Nontron to the prefect on the ramifications of the insurrection of 13 June 1849, dated 30 June 1849.

83. Obviously it would be useful to make a detailed study of the socialist-democrats' propaganda and organizing techniques. For Dordogne we have no studies comparable to those of Marcel Vigreux for Morvan, Raymond Huard for Gard, Maurice Agulhon for Var, and Michel Pigenet for Cher. But my purpose here is not to study the triumph of the Republic but to analyze the roots of antirepublican sentiment.

84. Yves-Marie Bercé has written several books on the roots of these attitudes.

85. Early in the Restoration the regime failed to keep its promise to abolish duties on wine, alcohol, tobacco, and salt, and people in the region were very sensitive to this issue. In July 1814, in Saint-Yriex, records of indirect taxes were burned and the vault was robbed. A month before Napoleon's return from Elba, shouts of "Long live the emperor!" and "Down with the Bourbons!" were heard in the small town of Aixe, not far from the Nontron district. See Ponteil, *La chute de Napoléon 1er,* pp. 127–128.

86. Rocal, "La Révolution de 1830," p. 329. Recall that it took Charles X two weeks to travel to Cherbourg.

87. Ibid., p. 332.

88. Report of the mayor of Sourzac, *Arch. Dép. Dordogne* 1 M 72.

89. On this affair see Rocal, *1848 en Dordogne,* vol. 2, pp. 14–15. Also, Ozouf, "Entre la fête et l'émeute," notes that the maypole and gallows exchanged meanings in 1789 and 1790.

90. Rocal, *1848 en Dordogne,* vol. 2, p. 18.

91. See Suzanne Coquerelle, "L'armée et la répression dans les campagnes (1848)," *Bibliothèque de la Révolution de 1848* 18 (1955): 121–159. See also Rémy Gossez, "La résistance à l'impôt: Les quarante-cinq centimes," *Bibliothèque de la Révolution de 1848* 15 (1953): 89–135, according to which the *départements* most deeply involved were Creuse, Corrèze, Charente-Inférieure, Lot, Tarn-et-Garonne, Lot-et-Garonne, Haute-Garonne, Gers, and Hautes-Pyrénées. I would add Dordogne to the list.

92. Rocal, *1848 en Dordogne,* vol. 2, p. 25.

93. Reported in the *Echo de Vesone,* 20 June 1848, and quoted by Rocal, *1848 en Dordogne,* vol. 1, p. 156.

94. Rocal, *1848 en Dordogne,* vol. 2, p. 9.

95. Ibid., vol. 1, p. 171.

96. So far as I know, there is no worthwhile study of this episode.

97. For a detailed analysis, see Alain Corbin, *Archaïsme et modernité*, vol. 1, pp. 502–510.
98. Jean-Baptiste Chavoix, *Proposition au sujet de l'impôt de 45 centimes* (Paris: Imprimerie de l'Assemblée Nationale, 1849), *Bibliothèque Nationale* Le 67 2.
99. *Arch. Nat.* BB30 359; also for the Saint-Félix affair.
100. This was previously pointed out in Philippe Vigier, *Le bonapartisme/ Der Bonapartismus* (Artemis: Munich, 1977), p. 15.
101. The tireless Jean-Baptiste Chavoix again proposed reimbursement of the 45 centimes on 12 March 1851. He also proposed an amendment to the law of 3 March 1844 concerning hunting.
102. In discussing the insurrection of December 1851, Maurice Agulhon described the role played by disparities in the political representations of the period in different social milieus.
103. Systematic analysis of archival documents concerning incidents connected with the practice of universal suffrage under the Second Republic reveals the importance of this problem. See Didier Portès, "La pratique du suffrage universel sous la Seconde République (2 mars 1848–31 mai 1850) à la lumière des archives judiciaires" (diss., University of Paris I, 1989). This work points out the effects of rumor, challenges, and folkways on the process of adaptation to universal suffrage.
104. Corbin, *Archaïsme et modernité*, vol. 1, p. 509. An allusion to the five-member executive commission that succeeded the provisional government installed in February 1848.
105. This and the subsequent quote are from the report of the subprefect of Nontron, 22 March 1852, *Arch. Nat.* F1 c III Dordogne 7; emphasis added.
106. Corbin, *Archaïsme et modernité*, vol. 2, p. 840.
107. Recall that on 2 December 1851, the president of the Republic staged a coup d'état that resulted in the arbitrary dissolution of the assembly elected on 13 May 1849, and at the same time reestablished universal male suffrage, which had been abolished by the law of 31 May 1850.
108. See the admirable book by Ted Margadant, *French Peasants in Revolt: The Insurrection of 1851* (Princeton: Princeton University Press, 1979). The only form of resistance that Margadant mentions in Dordogne was a demonstration by a hundred or so people aimed at obtaining the release of prisoners held in the town of Bergerac (ibid., p. 17).
109. When the peasants who were assembled on the fairground at Saint-Yriex learned of the fall of the July Monarchy and the establishment of a republic, they had little reaction and continued to go about their

business as before. See the subprefect's report cited in Corbin, *Archaïsme et modernité,* vol. 2, p. 705.

110. Rocal, *1848 en Dordogne,* vol. 2, pp. 211–212.

111. See Patrick Lacoste, "Les républicains en Dordogne au début de la IIIe République, 1870–1877" (diss., directed by André-Jean Tudesq, 1971), p. 23. Five of the ten republican candidates for election to the National Assembly on 8 February 1871, including those at the head of the list, had previously been elected to the Constituent Assembly in 1848 or to the Legislative Assembly in 1849.

112. Abundant information on this campaign, too tedious to spell out in detail here, can be found in *Arch. Nat.* BB18 1795 and BB18 1786, and in *Arch. Dép. Dordogne* 2 Z 73; there are also the periodic reports issued by prefects and *procureurs généraux.*

113. This failure, which contrasts with what Raymond Huard found in Gard (*Le mouvement républicain en Bas-Languedoc, 1848–1881* [Paris: Presses de la Fondation des Sciences Politiques, 1982], pp. 201–204), is particularly clear in the Nontron district, which was cut in two by the administration in a shrewd drawing of election precinct boundaries. According to the subprefect of Nontron, the partition had provoked discontent in the populace, and it was from this discontent that the opposition candidates drew most of their votes (*Arch. Dép.* 2 Z 73).

Consider the campaign of the *quarante-huitard* republican Jean-Baptiste Chavoix. (Welles de Lavalette, the candidate in the other precinct, ran unopposed.) Chavoix organized meetings, which the administration decided not to interfere with, at Lanouaille (twenty people at the home of a blacksmith and forty-odd others at the home of a tailor), Champagnac-de-Belair (twenty), Thiviers (twenty to thirty), Villars (a dozen), and Jumilhac-le-Grand (ninety). In this precinct—which included the Périgueux district, the city itself, and four cantons of the Nontron district—the official candidate, Paul Dupont, received 22,136 votes and the republican Jean-Baptiste Chavoix 10,872. In the third precinct, which included the Ribérac district and the other four cantons of the Nontron district, Welles de Lavalette, the only candidate, received 21,441 votes out of a total of 33,151 registered voters.

114. In this *département* there were 115,099 votes in favor, 10,653 opposed. See *Arch. Nat.* F1 c III Dordogne 7.

115. See Corbin, *Archaïsme et modernité,* vol. 2, pp. 904–906.

116. This was the finding of the *procureur général* of the court of Bordeaux, report of 12 January 1870, *Arch. Nat.* BB30 390.

117. Repeatedly mentioned in administrative reports.

118. On the importance of political choice to the peasant's sense of identity, see Pierre Vallin, *Paysans rouges du Limousin* (Paris: L'Harmattan, 1985), which shows how important socialist allegiances were to the formation of the identity of the Limousin peasant.

119. Robert Pimienta, in *La propagande bonapartiste en 1848* (Paris: Cornély, 1911), has analyzed these means of propaganda very carefully, but his purpose was not to trace the progress of rumor. See also André-Jean Tudesq, "La légende napoléonienne en France en 1848," *Revue historique* (July-September 1957): 64–85; Jean Tulard, *Napoléon ou le mythe du sauveur* (Paris: Fayard, 1983); and, with a different slant, Frédéric Bluche, *Le bonapartisme, aux origines de la droite autoritaire* (Paris: Nouvelles Editions Latines, 1980).

120. See Bernard Ménager, *Les Napoléon du peuple* (Paris: Aubier, 1988).

121. See Dominique Aubry, *Quatre-vingt-treize et les Jacobins: Regards littéraires du XIXe siècle* (Lyons: Presses Universitaires de Lyon, 1988), esp. pp. 224–233.

122. Pointed out by Bernard Ménager and confirmed by the master's theses of Emmanuelle Huyghes and Valérie Sekula (University of Paris I, 1989).

123. Rocal, "La Révolution de 1830," p. 213.

124. This argument has been developed by Philippe Vigier and draws on various works he edited.

125. Two recent theses, by François Pairault on Charente and Maurice Mathieu on Vienne, have gone some way toward compensating for the historical profession's neglect of democratic Caesarism. Some time ago Patrice Higonnet noted, with some surprise, the overwhelming support and unswerving loyalty that the peasants of Pont-de-Montvert (Lozère) offered to an imperial regime they did not perceive as "reactionary." See his *Pont-de-Montvert: Social Structure and Politics in a French Village, 1700–1914* (Cambridge, Mass.: Harvard University Press, 1971), pp. 121–124.

126. On this question see the special issue of *Revue d'histoire moderne et contemporaine: L'historiographie du Second Empire* 21 (January-March 1974).

127. Especially, as we shall see later on, Louis Mie and Charles Ponsac in Périgueux and Alcide Dusolier in Nontron. See *Ce que j'ai vu du 7 août 1870 au 1er février 1871* (Paris: Ernest Leroux, 1874), p. 18.

128. Is there any need to point out that Karl Marx immediately recognized the significance of this vote as a statement of identity?

129. Report of 26 December 1852, Arch. Nat. F1 c III Dordogne 7.

130. Letter from the mayor of Monfaucon, 22 November 1852, *Arch. Dép. Dordogne* 1 M 72, and report cited by the subprefect of Non-

tron, 26 December 1852, *Arch. Nat.* F1 c III Dordogne 7. Concerning the popular celebration at the end of 1851, see documents in *Arch. Nat.* F1 c III Dordogne 7—for example, the report by the subprefect of Bergerac, 1 February 1852. "Napoleonic banquets" were held in many communes, and congratulatory declarations were too numerous to be counted. See also the report of the subprefect of Nontron, 27 January 1852.

131. In contrast to what took place in some regions in the spring of 1848, the celebration in the Nontron district did not last long. There was nothing comparable to the outpourings of joy that occurred in 1830 (July to December), in 1851, and again in 1852.

132. Terms used by the subprefect of Nontron in his report 22 March 1852 (*Arch. Nat.* F1 c III Dordogne 7). Historians have not paid sufficient attention to this "administrative language" and its resonances with "the Napoleonic conception of campaigns" (also expressions used by the subprefect of Nontron).

133. Report of the prefect of Dordogne, 13 August 1869, *Arch. Nat.* F1 c III Dordogne 7. It would also be interesting to study the way in which imperial government officials thought of peasants. We should take care not to be misled by this configuration of social images.

134. This was one of the headings on the printed forms that *procureurs généraux* used in filing their reports.

135. Typical, in this respect, was the action of the prefect of Dordogne in 1868, and the grounds he gave. See report to the minister of the interior, 9 July 1868, *Arch. Nat.* F1 c III Dordogne 11. In a series of lectures he tried to demonstrate the importance of education for "the conservative interests of society as a whole." To that end, in 1868 the prefect established a Society for the Development of Primary Education in Dordogne.

136. To borrow the celebrated words of Adolphe Thiers (1864).

137. Regular reports of the cantonal commissioners, Nontron district, 1858–1869, *Arch. Dép. Dordogne* 2 Z 121.

138. Earlier I pointed out the importance of this phenomenon in nearby Limousin. See also Gabriel Désert, "Les paysans du Calvados, 1815–1895" (diss., University of Lille III, 1975).

139. The emphasis is that of the officials drafting the reports.

140. The backwardness of Dordogne in comparison to other areas such as Normandy is obvious here.

141. This was indeed quite late, since it dates from 1861. See *Arch. Dép. Dordogne* 7 M 59.

142. See Armengaud, *Les populations de l'Est-aquitaine*, pp. 420–421.

143. Procureur général, 11 January 1868 and especially 7 April 1868. In

Mussidan, for example, youths welcomed the subprefect with shouts of "Vive la Mobile!" See *Arch. Nat.* BB30 374, and prefect, 7 March 1868, in *Arch. Nat.* F1 c III Dordogne 7.

144. *Procureur général,* July 1859, *Arch. Nat.* BB30 374.

145. As implied by the title of the national anthem, which deserves to be taken seriously.

146. The possibility that Camille de Maillard showed sympathy for the republicans should not be totally discounted. One can imagine that this ebullient young legitimist believed it might be easier for him to win a hearing for his ideas and play a political role in a republic prepared to accept universal suffrage, as in 1849, than under an empire that kept a tight rein on aristocratic supporters of Henri V.

2. Anxiety and Rumor

1. Thanks to the diligence of prefects, prosecutors, and police, we can accurately reconstruct the vicissitudes of public opinion from 15 July 1870, when the conflict began, to 16 August 1870, when Alain de Monéys was murdered. Note that although the decision to declare war was made on July 15, Prussia was not officially notified until July 19.

2. Report from the prefect to the Ministry of the Interior, 6 August 1870, *Arch. Nat.* F1 c III Dordogne 7.

3. Despite this resigned anticipation, the declaration of war seems to have surprised most people in the countryside. See Audoin-Rouzeau, *1870,* pp. 48ff.; and idem, "Le sentiment national en France pendant la guerre de 1870," *Bulletin de la Société d'Histoire Moderne,* series 16, no. 42 (1989): 11.

4. The expressions quoted appear in Audoin-Rouzeau, "Le sentiment national," p. 11.

5. Faury, *Cléricalisme et anticléricalisme dans le Tarn, 1848–1900,* p. 85.

6. Audoin-Rouzeau, *1970,* p. 67. Information of a general nature in the following pages is taken largely from this book.

7. Report of prefect, 6 August 1870.

8. Report of *procureur général,* August 1870, cited by Faury, *Cléricalisme et anticléricalisme dans le Tarn, 1848–1900,* pp. 87–88.

9. See Claude Farenc, "Guerre, information et propagande en 1870–1871: Le cas de la Champagne," *Revue d'histoire moderne et contemporaine* 31 (January–March 1984).

10. Audoin-Rouzeau, *1870,* pp. 112–113.

11. As mayor Elie Mondout recalled in September. See *Arch. Dép. Dordogne* 1 M 41.

12. On August 9, the prefect of Charente, the *département* bordering the commune of Hautefaye, wrote: "The local national guard does not exist here and the mobile guard has not yet been organized." *Arch. Nat.* F7 12660. On August 20, the prefect of Dordogne sent a dispatch to the Ministry of the Interior: "No local national guard, no rifles." *Service Historique de l'Armée de Terre* La8. From responses to a ministerial memo of August 16, it appears that the mobile guard was in roughly the same shape throughout the region. See responses of the prefects of Gironde, Charente (August 17), and Dordogne (August 20).

13. The *procureur général* singled out the "emotion caused by the general levy" as the major cause of the tragedy (dispatch to minister of justice from Nontron, August 19, *Service Historique de l'Armée de Terre* La8). On August 13 the "local news" column of *Le Nontronnais* described the enthusiasm of the volunteers and the joy of the crowd applauding them on the town square of Nontron.

14. Audoin-Rouzeau, *1870,* pp. 128–129.

15. Report of prefect, *Arch. Nat.* F7 12660.

16. Report of prefect, 6 August 1870.

17. Audoin-Rouzeau, *1870,* p. 135.

18. Prefect to minister of the interior, 15 March 1869; Louis Mie spoke to an audience of three hundred at a meeting in Périgueux during the election campaign. *Arch. Nat.* BB18 1795.

19. Dusolier, *Ce que j'ai vu,* pp. 7–16.

20. See Patrick de Ruffray, *L'affaire de Hautefaye: Légende, histoire* (Angoulême, 1926), p. 22.

21. Pointed out by Jean-Louis Galet, *Meurtre à Hautefaye* (Périgueux: Fanlac, 1970), p. 30.

22. See Dusolier, *Ce que j'ai vu,* p. 20. For further details, see Audoin-Rouzeau, *1870,* passim.

23. Faury, *Cléricalisme et anticléricalisme,* p. 87. See also Philip Hamerton, *Round My House* (Boston, 1885), p. 213; quoted in Weber, *Peasants.*

24. *L'Echo de Châtellerault* and *Le Courrier de la Vienne,* quoted in *Le Charentais,* 18 August 1870. Three days later, it was rumored at the railroad station that 11,000 rifles had been shipped to Prussia by treasonous Frenchmen. Allegedly seized at the border, they were supposed to have been sent to Châtellerault. The subprefect had to intervene. In fact, the weapons were being sent to "La Manufacture" for repair.

25. "Notices paroissiales," box 11, *Archives de l'Evêché de Poitiers*. I am indebted to Maurice Mathieu for this information.

26. Dossier of Gabriel Palus, *Arch. Dép. Dordogne* J 1431, note by the author of the dossier.

27. Dossier of Gabriel Palus.

28. Président M. Simonet, *La tragédie du 16 août 1870 à Hautefaye* (Bordeaux: Siraudeau, 1929), p. 6.

29. Dusolier, *Ce que j'ai vu*, p. 19. The same report can be found in the 18 August 1870 entry of the Chambon brothers' *Notes et souvenirs*, quoted in Gibson, "Les notables," vol. 1, p. 258.

30. This and subsequent quotes are from the *procureur impérial* of Ribérac to the *procureur général*, 18 August 1870. Document reproduced in Georges Marbeck, *Cent documents autour du drame de Hautefaye* (Périgueux: Pierre Fanlac, 1983), p. 74.

31. This strategy is clearly explained in Maurice Mathieu's thesis on Vienne. In 1871 Charles Ponsac discussed it in *Le crime de Hautefaye* (Bordeaux: Imprimerie Viéville et Capiomont, 1871).

32. Simonet, *La tragédie du 16 août 1870 à Hautefaye*, p. 6.

33. Dusolier, *Ce que j'ai vu*, p. 19.

34. See Olender, in *Le genre humain 5* (1982), special issue entitled *La rumeur* (Paris: Fayard, 1982), p. 9. Michel-Louis Rouquette discusses the many functions of rumor, which not only "reveals psychosocial identities" but also proposes solutions to ill-defined problems. See Rouquette, "La rumeur comme résolution d'un problème mal défini," *Cahiers internationaux de sociologie* 86 (1989): 117–122. The quote is from p. 118.

35. See Lydia Flem, *La rumeur*, p. 12, on the work of Gordon Allport and Leo Postman, especially their book *The Psychology of Rumor* (New York: Henry Holt, 1947).

36. Ibid., pp. 15–16; analysis of the work of Floyd Allport and Milton Lepkin.

37. The revelation of the Hautefaye crime did not silence the rumors. In the October 20 issue of *Le Nontronnais*, a resident of Javerlhac denied having started a rumor that Colonel Albert Moreau de Saint-Martin had transmitted money to the Prussians. This story is reported without a reference in Georges Marbeck, *Hautefaye: L'année terrible* (Paris: Robert Laffont, 1982), p. 325.

38. Dossier of Gabriel Palus, *Arch. Dép. Dordogne* J 1431.

39. See Eliane de Rigaud, "La fête du roi sous la monarchie de Juillet" (diss., University of Paris I, October 1989).

40. See Mathieu Truesdell, "La Révolution française et ses reflets dans les célébrations officielles du Second Empire," *L'image de la Révolution*

française, vol. 3, pp. 2147–2152. This national holiday was not confined to France. In 1858 and 1860 the fifteenth of August was celebrated as a holiday by Italians in favor of national unity as a way of honoring the principle of nationality. See Hélène Bureau, "L'image de l'Italie et des Italiens à travers la correspondance politique des consuls de France en Italie" (diss., University of Paris I, June 1989), pp. 183–184.

41. See Ménager, *Les Napoléon du peuple,* pp. 153–157; and Udo Zembol, "La fête du 15 août sous le Second Empire" (diss., University of Paris I, October 1989). See also René Boudard, "La célébration de la fête de l'empereur sous le Second Empire," *Mémoires de la Société des Sciences Naturelles et Archéologiques de la Creuse* 31 (1953): 436–444.

42. See the abundant correspondence of mayors on this subject, *Arch. Dép. Dordogne* 1 M 96. Subsequent examples and quotes are taken from this dossier.

43. I refer to the "mayoralty" as institution; many rural communes in the Nontron district are without an actual town hall.

44. In 1869, for example.

45. This was of course a way of identifying opponents, who lit no lights.

46. See Rosemonde Sanson, *Les 14 juillet, 1789–1975: Fête et conscience nationale* (Paris: Flammarion, 1976).

47. In Saint-Astier, bells were rung for half an hour on 14 August 1865.

48. The cited dossier in the *archives départementales* unfortunately contains no information about the August 15 celebration in Hautefaye.

49. Such was the opinion of the fair's chief proponents. See *Arch. Dép. Dordogne* 8 M 14 for an accurate map of the Hautefaye fair's drawing power. See also map in the frontmatter of this book.

50. Unfortunately there is no work covering the period 1815–1870 comparable to Dominique Margairaz's study of the end of the Ancien Régime, the Revolution, and the Empire: *Foires et marchés dans la France préindustrielle* (Paris: Ecole des Hautes Etudes en Sciences Sociales, 1988). Note that Dordogne was part of a region in which fairs were densely distributed and that their number grew from the year III (1794) onward. Between 1770 and 1820, the growth was most noticeable in livestock fairs. Gibson (*Les notables,* vol. 2, p. 179) cites *Le calendrier de la Dordogne* for 1847, according to which there were at that time apparently 135 fairs in the *département.* But this source seems to list only the largest ones.

51. Table found in the same dossier as a letter from the subprefect of Nontron to the mayor of Hautefaye, 18 July 1821, *Arch. Dép. Dordogne* 8 M 14.

52. Many fairs served as collection points for livestock, which were then funneled into commercial channels. See Margairaz, *Foires et marchés dans la France préindustrielle*, p. 147.

53. Three-day fairs were relatively rare at the end of the Ancien Régime (ibid., p. 90). Several reports, including that of young Villard, clearly indicate that the fair was not limited to August 16, although this was the officially accredited date.

54. Letter from Hautefaye notables and petition of local mayors to the ministry, 1 May 1836, *Arch. Dép. Dordogne* 8 M 14.

55. Record of municipal deliberations of the commune of Hautefaye, 29 March 1869, *Arch. Dép. Dordogne* E deposit.

56. Isac Chiva, "Les places marchandes et le monde rural," *Foires et marchés ruraux en France: Etudes rurales* (April–December 1980): 7.

57. Margairaz, *Foires et marchés dans la France préindustrielle*, pp. 203ff., emphasizes that these gatherings had great importance in the minds of small landowners.

58. We do not know if *accordeurs* (intermediaries whose role was to facilitate deals) were present on the fairground of Hautefaye.

59. Compare the celebrations that accompanied the agricultural association's competition in Nontron on 14 September 1862 (*Arch. Dép.* 7 M 59). At night almost the whole town was lit up. The Italian café stood out with its splendid lighting. A huge allegorical transparency decorated the façade of the town hall. Fireworks lit up the night sky prior to the beginning of "a dance of the sort seen only in Nontron." Clearly, peasants would have felt more at home on the fairground at Hautefaye, even those keen to win the badge of honor that was awarded for the plowing contest the following morning, prior to the agricultural association Mass.

60. See report of M. Villars, 9 October 1870 (*Arch. Dép. Dordogne* 1 M 41).

61. The subprefect of Nontron pointed this out in 1821 (*Arch. Dép. Dordogne* 8 M 14).

62. Margairaz, *Foires et marchés dans la France préindustrielle*, p. 142, notes that these existed at the end of the eighteenth century: "Many agricultural meetings were held in tiny villages, sometimes unreachable by anything wider than a small path."

63. Annual summary, *Arch. Nat.* F7 3981.

64. Some of these fairs would survive—for example, the one studied by Christian Zarka in the hamlet of Hérolles, near Bellac. See Zarka, "Les fonctions marchandes et leurs traces dans le paysage," in *Foires et marchés ruraux,* pp. 253ff. This essay deals with a fair similar in

many respects to that of Hautefaye, and I learned a great deal from
it.

65. Report of 16 April 1853 (probably from the gendarmerie), *Arch. Nat.*
F1 c III Dordogne 11.

66. Report of gendarmerie, 12 May 1853, ibid.

67. Note from the Ministry of the Interior, 27 May 1853, ibid.

68. On the rituals associated with regional livestock fairs around the turn
of the century, see Marie-Claude Groshens, "La fin des foires et la
persistance des marchés en Périgord," *Foires et marchés ruraux,*
pp. 176ff.

69. Chiva, "Les places marchandes et le monde rural," p. 7.

70. See Pierre Lamaison, "Des foires et des marchés en Haute-Lozère,"
in *Foires et marchés ruraux,* pp. 199 ff.

71. Urban fairs provided an opportunity for peasants to visit prostitutes.
See Alain Corbin, *Les filles de noce* (Paris: Aubier, 1978), pp. 224ff.,
published in English as *Women for Hire: Prostitution and Sexuality
in France after 1850* (Cambridge, Mass.: Harvard University Press,
1990); and Jacques Termeau, *Maisons closes de province* (Le Mans:
Editions Cénomane, 1986), p. 185. The same was true in York,
according to Frances Finnegan.

72. In an oral survey of agricultural conditions conducted in 1866, notables were vehemently critical of fairs for all these reasons.

73. Of ninety-one brawls and riots in Lot villages between 1815 and
1850, forty-three (45 percent) took place on fairgrounds. Dordogne
seems to have been much less affected by this scourge than the
northeastern part of the neighboring *département,* which was subject
to cycles of vendetta. See François Ploux, "Les bagarres de villages
(1815–1850): Contribution à l'étude des formes collectives de la
violence en milieu rural" (diss., University of Paris I, 1989).
Margairaz, *Foires et marchés dans la France préindustrielle,* p. 205,
also points out that fairs were a focal point of violence in the eighteenth century.

74. The fair was part of the "drinking culture" that has been studied by
a group of historians led by Susanna Barrows, at the University of
California, Berkeley.

75. Indicated by the *procureur général,* 1859 (*Arch. Nat.,* BB30 374). The
authorities even ordered the closing of a Nontron café where considerable sums of money were lost on fair and market days.

76. Pointed out by Zarka, "Les fonctions marchandes," p. 254, in the
case of the Hérolles fair.

77. Report of prefect, 7 June 1870, *Arch. Nat.* F1 c III Dordogne 7.

78. The regional press devoted a series of articles to the problem; these were collected by Gabriel Palus in *Arch. Dép.* J 1431. See, for example, *L'Echo de la Dordogne* (issues of June 10, 24, 25, and July 2). The quotation is taken from the June 6 issue. *Le Nontronnais* also reported on the problem; see the June 11 issue in Marbeck, *Cent documents,* p. 53.

79. Report of 9 July 1870, *Arch. Nat.* BB30 390.

80. Chiva, "Les places marchandes et le monde rural," p. 10.

81. Ibid., p. 11.

82. See Maurice Robert, ed., *Limousin et Limousins: Image régionale et identité culturelle* (Limoges: Souny, 1988); and, for the failure of the inverse process in historical perspective, Caroline Girard, "Des mangeurs de châtaignes aux bâtisseurs de la Nation: La fabrication d'une contre-image limousine" (diss., University of Paris I, 1989).

83. Oral survey of agriculture, 1866, quoted in Marbeck, *Cent documents,* p. 10.

84. See Corbin, *Archaïsme et modernité,* passim.

85. See René Collignon, *Anthropologie de la France: Dordogne, Charente, Corrèze, Creuse, Haute-Vienne* (Paris: Société d'Anthropologie de Paris, 1894).

86. Edmond Demolins, *Les Français d'aujourd'hui: Les types sociaux du Midi et du Centre* (Paris: Firmin Didot, 1898).

87. The most recent book on the Lafarge affair is Laure Adler, *L'amour à l'arsenic: Histoire de Marie Lafarge* (Paris: Denoël, 1986).

88. Gibson, "Les notables," vol. 1, p. 259. The author refers to documents in *Arch. Dép. Dordogne* 63 P.

89. Details furnished by the temporary mayor, Elie Mondout, 22 September 1870, *Arch. Dép. Dordogne* 1 M 41.

90. File in *Arch. Dép. Dordogne* 12 O Hautefaye.

91. *Arch. Dép. Dordogne* 2 U 174, "Fratricide in Hautefaye," December 1841.

92. *Arch. Dép. Dordogne* 1 M 41.

93. R. Laugardière, "Essais topographiques, historiques et biographiques sur l'arrondissement de Nontron, commune de Hautefaye," *Bulletin de la Société Historique et Archéologique du Périgord* (November–December 1888): 403–408.

94. Information contained in two files concerning municipal elections, *Arch. Dép. Dordogne* 2 Z 75 and 76.

95. Note, however, that although six of the municipal councillors of Hautefaye were members of the agricultural society of Nontron at its founding in 1861, the following year none of them received any prize or bonus (*Arch. Dép. Dordogne* 7 M 59).

96. Ponsac, *Le crime d'Hautefaye.*
97. Gibson, "Les notables," vol. 1, p. 299.
98. *Arch. Dép. Dordogne* 12 O Hautefaye.
99. Hautefaye, Record of municipal deliberations, *Arch. Dép. Dordogne* E deposit.
100. *Arch. Dép. Dordogne* 2 T 27, quoted in Gibson, "Les notables," vol. 1, p. 259.
101. Brochure of the Société pour le Développement de l'Enseignement Primaire dans la Dordogne, 1869. *Arch. Nat.* F1 c III Dordogne 11.
102. Marbeck, *Cent documents*, p. 15. For a comparison with nearby *départements*, see maps by Corbin in E. R. Labande, ed., *Histoire du Poitou, du Limousin et des pays charentais* (Toulouse: Privat, 1976), pp. 418–419.
103. Gibson, "Les notables," vol. 2, p. 353.
104. Information taken from record of municipal deliberations (here and in the ensuing argument).
105. The priest was actually assigned the rank of *desservant* (below that of curé), but locals regarded him as a curé.
106. According to the cantonal commissioner (1 November 1864), the municipality kept good records and posted government notices as required (*Arch. Dép. Dordogne* 2 Z 121).
107. Marbeck, *Cent documents*, p. 49. Alain Bressy points out (ibid., p. 123) that the only republican in Hautefaye, a man by the name of Rougier, was unable to go to the polling place. The people of Beaussac also voted unanimously for the emperor. By contrast, 181 of 821 ballots in Nontron were marked "no."
108. *Arch. Dép.* 2 Z 121.
109. *Echo de la Dordogne*, Monday, 7 November 1870.
110. See Anne-Marie Sohn, "Les attentats à la pudeur sur les fillettes en France, 1870–1939, et la sexualité quotidienne," in *Violences sexuelles: Mentalités* 3 (October 1989): 71–111.
111. Except in the case of village brawls, but these were no longer common in 1870. According to Ploux, "Les bagarres," they began to go out of fashion in the 1840s.

3. The Celebration of Murder

1. More information on the senior Monéys can be found in the dossier assembled by Gabriel Palus, *Arch. Dép. Dordogne* J 1431; and in Ruffray, *L'affaire de Hautefaye*, pp. 41ff.
2. *Arch. Dép. Dordogne* 2 Z 76. Alain de Monéys led all other candidates in these elections, with 118 votes compared to only 57 for the

last of the municipal councillors. At this time the income on his fortune was evaluated at 4,000 francs, which implies that his family was not one of the wealthiest in the region. The Palus dossier contains a portrait of Alain de Monéys as well as photographs of family members.

3. According to Galet, *Meurtre à Hautefaye,* pp. 15ff. Unfortunately the author cites no sources.

4. Recall that on 8 May 1870, everyone in Beaussac voted "yes" in the plebiscite.

5. It is important to understand these names. Each man had a nickname, which was the name by which he was usually called. These nicknames were often revealing, and that is why I give them here. They could suggest a man's age, physical characteristics, moral qualities, or place of residence, especially in cases where a man married a well-to-do heiress.

6. To Camille de Maillard, the word *cartouches* (literally "cartridges") clearly meant "reserves." The peasants may not have understood the metaphorical use of the term.

7. All quotes in this chapter without explicit references are from the indictment and court minutes, which were published in 1871 by Charles Ponsac under the title *Le crime d'Hautefaye.* Repeated references to this work would have resulted in an inordinate number of notes.

8. Simonet, *La tragédie du 16 août 1870,* p. 10.

9. Note that in the two previous quotes, Alain de Monéys is clearly designated by name. But obviously by the time of the trial everyone knew the true identity of the victim, who was therefore no longer referred to as "the Prussian."

10. For further information see the dossier compiled by Gabriel Palus.

11. Prepared on 31 August 1870, and preserved in *Arch. Dép. Dordogne.* Reproduced in Marbeck, *Cent documents,* p. 70.

12. Ploux, "Les bagarres," p. 129, notes that in the case of village brawls, these were also rites of reconciliation.

13. The curé, aware of the empress's Catholic sentiments, inevitably hoped that her name would be hailed along with the emperor's.

14. Dossier cited, *Arch. Dép. Dordogne* J 1431.

15. Ponsac, *Le crime d'Hautefaye,* p. 2.

16. Feytou then "kicked him in the lower abdomen and referred to him as dead meat."

17. On the murder of young Chambert at Buzançais, see Yvon Bionnier, "Les jacqueries de 1847 en Bas-Berry" (diss., Tours, 1979); and

Philippe Vigier, *La vie quotidienne en province et à Paris pendant les journées de 1848* (Paris: Hachette, 1982), pp. 35–53.

18. On the murder of a gendarme named Bidan in Clamecy on 6 December 1851, see Marc Autenzio, "La résistance au coup d'état du 2 décembre 1851 dans la Nièvre" (diss., Tours, 1970); and Vigier, *La vie quotidienne,* pp. 319–327.

19. The massacre of fifty hostages is recounted in P. Duclos, "Une 'pétroleuse' convertie: Félicie Gimet et Pierre Olivaint," *Revue d'histoire de l'eglise de France* 74, no. 192 (January–June 1988): 53ff. This article contains a valuable bibliography.

20. Colin Lucas points out how cruel acts served as tests of virility during the White Terror; see Lucas, *Beyond the Terror: Essays in French Regional and Social History, 1794–1815* (Cambridge: Cambridge University Press, 1983), p. 170.

21. According to Camille de Maillard's niece Marguerite de Maillard, who was interviewed by Gabriel Palus in 1936 (see Palus dossier, *Arch. Dép. Dordogne*).

22. Ploux, "Les bagarres," p. 88. Some people claimed that the mayor allowed the murder to take place because the Monéys were not clients of his brother, the blacksmith of Beaussac. The truth of this speculation is extremely doubtful.

23. Minutes of deliberations of the Hautefaye commune, *Arch. Dép. Dordogne* E deposit.

24. Testimony of Campot senior.

25. Note that twice in our sources it is mentioned that the shout of "Vive l'Empereur!" was accompanied by raised hands.

26. Desvars junior, a hog dealer who spoke only dialect, testified that he clearly heard these words shouted.

27. Temporary mayor Elie Mondout claimed that the priest of Mainzac was present during the crime but that the residents of Hautefaye protected him from attack. Letter of 22 September 1870, *Arch. Dép. Dordogne* 1 M 41.

28. The peasants of the region were prone to violence. François Ploux, who has studied violent conflicts between village youths in the period 1815–1880, points out that 83 percent of these brawls took place south of a line joining Gascony to the Juras (see Ploux, "Les bagarres," p. 6). These fights were extraordinarily violent; 10 percent resulted in death. Government officials were astonished by the rioters' cruelty. Blows were directed primarily at the head, and there were no compunctions about hitting an enemy when he was down, indeed beating him to death. Young girls, old men, and solitary individuals

were among the primary targets of these young unmarried males, whose group violence helped cement village solidarity.

29. There was no need, given the peasants' skill at slaughtering animals. See Noélie Vialles, *Le sang et la chair: Les abattoirs des pays de l'Adour* (Paris: Maison des Sciences de l'Homme, 1987), p. 51. The author remarks that the word "killer," with its connotation of skill, did not sound as pejorative in the country as in the city.

30. Mathieu Murguet admitted having struck a blow with a pitchfork.

31. The word "lynching" comes from the name Charles Lynch, a Virginia judge reputedly quick to sentence defendants to summary execution by hanging. Needless to say, it is highly unlikely that any of the peasants at Hautefaye had ever heard of either the man or the practice.

32. Emmanuel Le Roy Ladurie used this expression in speaking of another period in his *Paysans de Languedoc* (Paris: Imprimerie Nationale, 1966), vol. 1, p. 503.

33. Because the assailants were unable to throw the body into a river, as the murderers of Marshal Brune did in 1815.

34. A common practice in Périgord.

35. At the trial, Philippe Dubois was the only witness to testify that wood was placed under the victim and that the body was covered with straw. In a study of Minot in Châtillonnais, Yvonne Verdier describes the treatment of a pig that has just been bled: it was "rolled onto a pile of small logs, covered with straw, and set on fire: the bristles and straw blazed up." See Yvonne Verdier, *Façons de dire, façons de faire: La laveuse, la couturière, la cuisinière* (Paris: Gallimard, 1979), p. 29.

36. Wearing his mayoral sash, he followed the procession everywhere. His presence may well have reassured the murderers.

37. Verdier, *Façons*, p. 29, writes that "the death agony was described and commented on in great detail." Yet at the same time "facetious words and acts . . . were associated with everything having to do with the hog from the time it was put to death up to the final meal" (p. 30).

38. On this procedure see (in addition to Verdier, *Façons*) Rolande Bonnain, "Le pêle-porc dans les Baronnies," in Isac Chiva, ed., *Les baronnies des Pyrénées* (Paris: Maison des Sciences de l'Homme, 1981), vol. 1, pp. 195–218. Hogs in the Baronnies are "peeled" with boiling water (p. 201), then seared. These procedures are performed by males on the first day of the slaughter. From records kept by Johannès Plantadis at the end of the nineteenth century (*Arch. Dép. Corrèze* 11 F 32), it is possible to gain some idea of how peasants in the remote district of Nontron might have gone about the task of

slaughtering hogs. This file also contains interesting information on fairs.

39. Verdier, *Façons*, pp. 24–25, reports that in the Nontron district "as a hog fattened it was honored with name and title: Monsieur Habillé de Soies [Mr. Bristly]." Verdier also reports on the contrast between "the rather giddy pleasure at the sight of massive bloodshed and the horror at the thought of burning the animal alive" (pp. 28–29). Lard and fatback were the primary cooking fats in the Nontron district.

40. Note, however, that the crowd did not fall upon the corpse after it was burned, as was customary in earlier massacres.

41. See dispatch to minister of justice, *Service Historique de l'Armée de Terre* La 8.

42. Both are in reports to the World Historical Congress, Moscow, 1970.

43. Georges Rudé, *The Crowd in the French Revolution* (Oxford: Oxford University Press, 1959). Rudé does, however, mention the importance of rumor and fears of conspiracy (pp. 248–251).

44. Vendetta plays a fundamental role in Robert Muchembled, *La violence au village (XVe–XVIIe siècles* (Brepols, 1989), pp. 323ff.

45. On settling scores in rural nineteenth-century France, see Frédéric Chauvaud, "Tensions et conflits: Aspects de la vie rurale au XIXe siècle d'après les archives judiciaires—L'exemple de l'arrondissement de Rambouillet (1811–1871)" (diss., University of Paris X–Nanterre, January 1989).

46. It was because the gendarmes of Bédarieux were deemed unduly harsh that they were slaughtered one by one by insurgents who had set fire to the building in which they had taken refuge. See Margadant, *French Peasants in Revolt*, p. 280.

47. Raymond Verdier, ed., *La vengeance dans les sociétés extra-occidentales* (Paris: Editions Cujas, 1980), vol. 1, especially the article by Verdier entitled "Le système vindicatoire."

48. See Lucas, *Beyond the Terror*; and Lewis Gwynn, "La Terreur Blanche et l'application de la loi Decazes dans le département du Gard (1815–1817)," *Annales historiques de la Révolution française* 175, no. 36 (January–March 1964). The author points out how the Decazes Law was used as an instrument of vengeance in Gard (pp. 181–182). Old affairs were dredged up. Belated vengeance was exacted for the Nîmes "riot" of 1790. To understand political behavior in this particular region, study of the vendetta system is clearly essential.

49. See Gérard Courtois, "La vengeance, du désir aux institutions," in Courtois, ed., *La vengeance,* vol. 4.

50. According to Ploux, "Les bagarres," p. 9, the average age of those most prominently involved was twenty-seven.

51. To borrow the title of Richard Cobb's classic work, *The Police and the People: French Popular Protest, 1789–1820*.

52. For other parts of the world, see Pierre Barral's report to the World Historical Congress, Moscow, 1970 (Oxford: Clarendon Press, 1970).

53. Mikhail Bakhtin, *Rabelais and His World,* trans. Hélène Iswolsky (Cambridge, Mass.: MIT Press, 1968).

54. Though during the time that Monéys was in the sheepfold, one of his assailants yelled: "You've drunk your coffee in fine polished rooms, now we'll make you drink it in a barn."

55. Belief in a hidden enemy is, of course, an important spur to revolutionary movements.

56. Pierre Caron, *Les massacres de septembre* (Paris: Maison du Livre Français, 1935). Caron also took an interest in the Hautefaye affair. He tried in vain to find the records of the Périgueux trial.

57. Paul Nicolle, "Les meurtres politiques d'août–septembre 1792 dans le département de l'Orne: Etude critique," *Annales historiques de la Révolution française* 62 (March–April 1934): 97ff. In Bellême, for example, the abbé Portail, who refused to take the oath of allegiance to the new regime, was beaten with clubs and logs. His assailants invited onlookers to beat him as proof of their civic-mindedness. The body was decapitated and the head paraded about the city. A "mob of children" dragged the headless body along behind (p. 109).

58. On Limousin, see Corbin, *Archaïsme et modernité*, vol. 1. Marcel Vigreux also ascribes considerable importance to this phenomenon in his study of Morvan.

59. In this respect it stands out as antithetical to the abduction of children that took place in Paris in 1750. Arlette Farge and Jacques Revel, in their book *Logiques de la foule: L'affaire des enlèvements d'enfants— Paris, 1750* (Paris: Hachette, 1988), show that the violence of the time indicated that the people no longer loved their king.

60. I use the term "enlightened" because it is convenient, but in so doing I do not mean to imply that the peasants' behavior was irrational or that their attitudes were primitive.

61. Here the adjective takes on its full meaning. Some commentators on Napoleon III's *Vie de César* argue that nineteenth-century French history was a replay of Roman history. The end of the Republic was dominated by the conquering hero, Caesar–Napoleon I; this was followed by a period of construction, consolidation of grandeur, and prosperity under Augustus–Napoleon III. See Corinne Boudin,

"Napoléon III, César et la Gaule: Archéologie et images du pouvoir sous le Second Empire" (diss., University of Paris I, 1989).

62. On the structural function of violence, see Michel Maffesoli, *Essais sur la violence, banale et fondatrice* (Paris: Librairie des Méridiens, 1984), an interesting work that focuses on extreme situations and calls attention to the way in which violence can "collectivize" fate and thereby overcome isolation. His analysis can easily be applied to the Hautefaye mob. It also shows why historians must examine massacres if they hope to understand behavior whose only traces are stained with blood.

63. See the key article by Georges Lefebvre, "Les foules révolutionnaires," recently reprinted in *La grande peur de 1789* (Paris: Armand Colin, 1988). In an introduction to this volume, Jacques Revel surveys work in this difficult area, the emergence of mass psychology. Compare the very different analyses in Serge Moscovici, *L'age des foules: Un traité historique de psychologie des masses* (Paris: Fayard, 1981), and in Susanna Barrows, *Distorting Mirrors: Visions of the Crowd in Late Nineteenth-Century France* (New Haven: Yale University Press, 1981). And see also the classic work of Robert A. Nye, *The Origins of Crowd Psychology: Gustave Le Bon and the Crisis of Mass Democracy in the Third Republic* (London, 1975).

64. René Girard, *Des choses cachées depuis la fondation du monde* (Paris: Grasset, 1978), p. 163.

65. Girard himself has warned against interpreting recent events in the terms set out in his work. Still, Girard's ideas seem to me quite germane to the analysis of Hautefaye.

66. Girard, *Des choses cachées,* pp. 42 and 57.

4. Monstrous Brutes

1. Clearly it would be impossible to compress the history of massacre and reactions to massacre into the space available here. What follows is a summary of the main points of the work of a number of historians.

2. Le Roy Ladurie, *Les paysans de Languedoc;* idem, *Le carnaval de Romans: De la Chandeleur au mercredi des cendres, 1579–1580* (Paris: Gallimard, 1979); Frank Lestringant, "Catholiques et cannibales: Le thème du cannibalisme dans le discours protestant au temps des guerres de religion," in *Pratiques et discours alimentaires à la Renaissance* (Paris: Maisonneuve et Larose, 1982), pp. 233–247, from which the expressions in quotes are taken; and Denis Crouzet,

"La violence au temps des troubles de religion (vers 1525–vers 1610)" (diss., University of Paris IV, 1988).

3. Crouzet, "La violence," pp. 26, 123.

4. Ibid., pp. 217ff., 231ff.

5. Ibid., pp. 235 and 245.

6. Ibid., pp. 737 and 255–281.

7. See Janine Garrisson-Estèbe, *La Saint-Barthélemy* (Brussels and Paris: Complexe-PUF, 1987).

8. Crouzet, "La violence," p. 1017.

9. Ibid., p. 1567.

10. Le Roy Ladurie, *Les paysans de Languedoc,* vol. 1, pp. 391–415, 493–508, 605–629. See also the works cited by Yves-Marie Bercé, as well as Nicole Castan, *Les criminels de Languedoc: Les exigences d'ordre et les voies du ressentiment dans une société pré-révolutionnaire, 1750–1790* (Toulouse: Publications de l'Université de Toulouse–Le Mirail, 1980), particularly the analyses of "brutal instincts" in popular violence, resistance to suffering (pp. 196ff.), and the indifference of spectators to the sight of pain.

11. Michel Bée, "Le spectacle de l'exécution dans la France d'Ancien Régime," *Annales: Economies, sociétés, civilisations* 4 (July–August 1983): 847–848. See also Pieter Spierenburg, *The Spectacle of Suffering: Executions and the Evolution of Repression, from a Preindustrial Metropolis to the European Experience* (Cambridge: Cambridge University Press, 1984); and Thomas W. Laqueur, "Crowds, Carnival and the State in English Executions, 1604–1868," in *Great Britain— the First Modern Society: Essays in Honour of Laurence Stone* (Cambridge: Cambridge University Press, 1989).

12. Louis-Sébastien Mercier, quoted in Bée, "Le spectacle," p. 845. On the practice of torture in the Ancien Régime, see Arlette Farge, *La vie fragile, violence, pouvoirs et solidarités à Paris au XVIIIe siècle* (Paris: Hachette, 1986), pp. 206ff. See also the first issue (1988) of the journal *Mentalités*, a special issue titled *Affaires du sang*, with an introductory essay by Arlette Farge.

13. Le Roy Ladurie, *Les paysans de Languedoc,* vol. 1, pp. 608ff., on the growing restraint of Catholic behavior toward the end of the seventeenth century.

14. On this episode see Pierre Rétat, ed., *L'attentat de Damiens: Discours sur l'événement au XVIIIe siècle* (Lyon: Presses Universitaires de Lyon, 1979).

15. See the classic work by David Bakan, *Disease, Pain and Sacrifice: Toward a Psychology of Suffering* (Chicago: University of Chicago Press, 1968); and the admirable article by Jean-Pierre Peter, "Silence

et cris: La médecine devant la douleur, ou l'histoire d'une élision," *Le genre humain* 18 (Fall 1988): 177–194, which points out how doctors developed a precise rhetoric for describing pain and notes that surgeons worried that any attenuation of the patient's pain might threaten the prestige they derived from their heroic confrontation with suffering.

16. See Thomas W. Laqueur, "Bodies, Details and the Humanitarian Narrative," paper presented at Princeton University, Spring 1987.

17. See Julia Kristeva, *"Pouvoirs de l'horreur: Essai sur l'abjection"* (Paris: Editions du Seuil, 1980), esp. pp. 9–10, concerning the natural revulsion from "the sudden, overwhelming emergence of alien strangeness . . . , troubling, radically separate, disgusting . . . [even] unclean."

18. Farge, *La vie fragile,* p. 217.

19. Ibid., p. 210.

20. On these two processes, see the classic works of Michel Foucault, *Surveiller et punir: Naissance de la prison* (Paris: Gallimard, 1975), pp. 9–72, and *Naissance de la clinique* (Paris: Galilée, 1963).

21. On changes in the "forms of disgust," see Jean-Clément Martin, "Le sang impur de la Révolution," in *Mentalités* (1988), special issue titled *Affaires du sang.*

22. Bernard Conein, "Le tribunal et la terreur du 14 juillet 1789 aux massacres de septembre," *Les révoltes logiques* 11 (Winter 1979–1980): 7. The author has also written a thesis on this subject.

23. See Marc Richir, "La trahison des apparences," *Le genre humain* (Winter 1987–1988): 139–156.

24. Conein, "Le tribunal," p. 7.

25. On 16 July 1789, the heads of Flesselles and de Launay (murdered on the fourteenth), "wrapped in a rag attached to a stick," were presented to an assembly of electors at Saint-Roch Church. When the package was undone, the heads were held up by the hair and exhibited to the crowd, as at an execution. See ibid., p. 6.

26. Ibid., p. 9 (quoting *Le Moniteur,* vol. 14, p. 463).

27. Ibid., p. 10.

28. Bée, "Le spectacle," p. 857.

29. Daniel Arasse, *La guillotine et l'imaginaire de la Terreur* (Paris: Flammarion, 1987).

30. Mona Ozouf, "Guerre et terreur dans le discours révolutionnaire, 1792–1794," *La bataille, la gloire, 1745–1871* (Clermont-Ferrand: University of Clermont-Ferrand, 1985), vol. 1, pp. 288–289, examines the embarrassment of revolutionary leaders in the face of disturbing outbreaks of blind violence during the Revolution. The revolu-

tionaries, afraid that their cause would be stained by the bloodshed, responded with two kinds of tactics. Some, like Roland, attempted to draw a veil over the events and refused to talk about them. Others told edifying anecdotes intended to demonstrate the delicate sensibility of the revolutionaries. Still, the crucial point is that the outbreak of horror gave Danton and Robespierre the idea for the organization of the Terror, which they saw as a "fixation abscess" [that is, an abscess deliberately created for therapeutic purposes—*Trans.*].

31. The subject of a debate reported on by Arasse in *La guillotine.*

32. This may have been even more prevalent in England, despite the difference in the instrument of execution. The last words of the condemned are present throughout the classic work by Edward P. Thompson, *The Making of the English Working Class* (London: Gallancz, 1963).

33. Despite the many good books on this episode, especially those of Charles Tilly, Claude Petitfrère, and Jean-Clément Martin, and despite many collaborative investigations, we still have no anthropological study of the types of cruelty practiced in this conflict. Yet for the historian they are an object of particular interest, because they are expressions not only of Dionysiac mob instincts but also of individual sadism and early forms of mass murder. A soon-to-be-published book by Jean-Clément Martin should contribute to our understanding.

34. On the growing prevalence of the "cannibal" image, see Baczko, *Comment sortir de la Terreur,* pp. 288–304.

35. L. M. Prudhomme, *Histoire générale et impartiale des erreurs, des fautes et des crimes commis pendant la Révolution française* (1797), vol. 1, note to reader.

36. Ibid., p. iv.

37. Ibid., vol. 3, p. 149.

38. On these episodes, see the works by Henry Houssaye and Colin Lucas cited previously.

39. Peter, "Silence et cris."

40. I attempted to analyze this process briefly in Michelle Perrot, ed., *History of Private Life,* trans. Arthur Goldhammer (Cambridge, Mass.: Harvard University Press, 1990), vol. 4, pp. 421ff. Further information on the history of sensibility may be found in Daniel Teysseire, *De la vie dans les rapports du Physique et du Moral de l'homme de Cabanis* (Saint Cloud: Ecole Normale Supérieure, 1982). On Cabanis see Martin S. Staum, *Cabanis: Enlightenment and Medical Philosophy in the French Revolution* (Princeton: Princeton University Press, 1980).

41. On the medical community's reaction, see Marie-Jeanne Lavilatte-

Couteau, "L'anesthésie—un embarras éthique: Contribution à une histoire mentale de l'anesthésie, 1846–1850" (diss., Tours, 1987).

42. Also the quartering of animal carcasses. Parent-Duchâtelet examined the reform of both types of establishments: see, for example, his "Projet d'un rapport . . . sur la construction d'un clos central d'équarrissage pour la ville de Paris," *Hygiène publique* (Paris: J.-B. Baillière, 1836), vol. 2, pp. 320ff.; and idem, *Les chantiers d'équarrissage de la ville de Paris* (1832), passim.

43. Vialles, *Le sang et le chair,* pp. 15–16. According to Vialles, the word *abattoir* ("slaughterhouse") was first used in 1806. See also Noélie Vialles, "L'âme et la chair: Le sang des abattoirs," *Affaires de sang,* esp. p. 146, from which the quote is taken.

44. See Maurice Agulhon, "Le sang des bêtes," *Romantisme* 31 (1981).

45. See Louis Chevalier, *Classes laborieuses et classes dangereuses à Paris pendant la première moitié du XIXe siècle* (Paris: Plon, 1958), pp. 78–85.

46. Philippe Ariès, *L'homme devant la mort* (Paris: Editions du Seuil, 1977), published in English as *Images of Men and Death* (Cambridge, Mass.: Harvard University Press, 1985).

47. Parent-Duchâtelet, "De l'influence et de l'assainissement des salles de dissection," *Hygiène publique,* vol. 2, pp. 10ff. Jean-Claude Caron, "La jeunesse des écoles de Paris, 1815–1848" (diss., University of Paris I, 1989), vol. 1, pp. 267, 269–270, 312, 359, 432, analyzes the new sensibility, which ultimately castigated as intolerable the nonchalant attitudes of certain students toward body parts, which were sometimes dropped in the streets or taken home for later dissection. In December 1842 a student named Porcheron exhibited a child's arm on a vaudeville stage. For this act he was summoned to appear before the academic council on 3 May 1843.

48. See Allan Mitchell, "The Paris Morgue as a Social Institution in the Nineteenth Century," *Francia* 4 (1976): 581–596 and 992–993.

49. Norbert Elias, *La dynamique de l'Occident* (Paris: Calmann-Lévy, 1975), esp. p. 287 on the "instinct conditioning" of the bourgeoisie. Charles, Louise, and Richard Tilly, in their book *The Rebellious Century, 1830–1930* (Cambridge, Mass.: Harvard University Press, 1975), pp. 49–86, were the first to pay attention to changes in the nature of collective and political violence and its participants.

50. The inability to bear the sight of blood is related to the growing intolerance of strong animal odors. See Alain Corbin, *Le miasme et la jonquille: L'odorat et l'imaginaire social* (Paris: Aubier, 1982), published in English as *The Foul and the Fragrant: Odor and the French Social Imagination,* trans. Alan Sheridan (Cambridge, Mass.:

Harvard University Press, 1986). In another area, *Le Conseiller du Peuple* in June 1851 expressed outrage that people now "claimed the right to shout inside buildings, a right that was granted to men only when they lived in forests." Quoted in Pierre Michel, *Un mythe romantique: Les Barbares, 1789–1848* (Lyon: Presses Universitaires de Lyon, 1981), p. 306.

51. Rétat, *L'attentat*, p. 265.
52. Quoted in Michel, *Un mythe romantique*, p. 216.
53. Rétat, *L'attentat*, p. 265.
54. Georges Benrekassa, "Histoire d'un assassinat: La mort de Marat dans l'historiographie du XIXe siècle," in Jean-Claude Bonnet et al., *La mort de Marat* (Paris: Flammarion, 1986).
55. Ibid., p. 304.
56. To borrow a well-known phrase of Victor Hugo's. Guy Rosa's notes to Hugo's *Les misérables* (Paris: Livre de Poche, 1984) are very interesting in this regard.
57. Mario Praz, *La chair, la mort et le diable dans la littérature du XIXe siècle: Le romantisme noir* (Paris: Denoël, 1977), examines the way in which horror was discovered to be a source of pleasure and beauty. Praz points to Jules Janin's *L'âne mort* as an exemplar of the "carrion novel," which begins with a description of a slaughterhouse for horses and ends with the violation of a tomb (pp. 125–127). Praz examines the work of Petrus Borel from this point of view.
58. See Raoul Girardet, *La société militaire dans la France contemporaine, 1815–1939* (Paris: Plon, 1953), ch. 1; and two outstanding recent contributions to the subject by the Société d'Histoire de la Révolution de 1848 et des Révolutions du XIXe Siècle: *Maintien de l'ordre et polices en France et en Europe au XIXe siècle* (Paris: Créaphis, 1987), and *Répression et prison politiques au XIXe siècle* (Paris: Créaphis, 1990).
59. Recall that General Bonaparte dispersed a crowd of royalist demonstrators on 13 Vendémiaire, Year IV (of the revolutionary calendar).
60. There are many links between the prevalence of mass murder and the coming of the new age. The power of the July Monarchy, for example, was consolidated in its first four, bloody years. Both the Second Empire and the Third Republic began with the spilling of much blood, and even the Second Republic established its institutions in the wake of the massacre of June 1848.
61. See Baczko, *Comment sortir*, pp. 295ff.
62. Michel, *Un mythe romantique*, pp. 528ff., discusses procedures intended to create an ideal of the "good citizen," which became a fundamental ingredient of Bonapartism.

63. For a long time, social observers were motivated by a desire to give substance to this distinction.

64. David Pinkney, *The French Revolution of 1830* (Princeton: Princeton University Press, 1972); and John E. Talbott, "The Good Workingman: Image and Reality in the Revolutions of 1830 and 1848," *Missouri Honors Review,* vol. 1, pp. 51–55. On the fear of numbers, the inversion of images of the people, and the exorcism of "recurrent barbarism," see Pierre Rosanvallon, *Le moment Guizot* (Paris: Gallimard, 1985), pp. 83ff.

65. See Stéphane Massy, "La commémoration du dixième anniversaire de la révolution de Juillet (28 juillet 1840)" (diss., University of Paris I, 1988).

66. See Mark Traugott, "The Crowd in the French Revolution of February 1848," *American Historical Review* 93, no. 3 (June 1988): 638–652.

67. This intention is plainly evident in Alexis de Tocqueville's *Souvenirs.* On this episode see Mark Traugott, *Armies of the Poor: Determinants of Working-Class Participation in the Partisan Insurrection of June 1848* (Princeton: Princeton University Press, 1985).

68. Vigier, *La vie quotidienne,* pp. 325 and 422.

69. Mark Traugott, a good analyst of the violence of 1848, is working on a book about barricades in Paris. He, too, has been struck by the thoroughness with which all traces of the massacre were effaced. Little if anything is known about the violence of the June 1848 insurrection. The history of that event, which has had more influence than any other on social and political representations, has been based on statistics, rumors hastily dismissed as without foundation, and incautious use of fictional accounts. Hugo's *Les misérables* (about violence early in the July Monarchy) and Flaubert's *L'éducation sentimentale* (about the revolution of February 1848) give stirring but questionable accounts of these crucial periods.

70. On fear of monsters, see my essay in *History of Private Life,* vol. 4, pp. 615ff.

71. Jean-Pierre Peter, "Ogres d'archives," *Nouvelle revue de psychanalyse* 6 (Fall 1972).

72. Michel Foucault, ed., *Moi, Pierre Rivière, qui ai égorgé ma mère, ma soeur, mon frère* (Paris: Gallimard, 1975), pp. 249ff.

73. On the stir caused by the event in provincial and Paris newspapers, see Clarisse Schweitzer, "Le Radeau de la Méduse et l'opinion publique" (diss., University of Paris I, 1988).

74. Ploux, "Les bagarres," pp. 116ff.

75. Canler, *Mémoires* (Paris: Mercure de France, 1968), pp. 268–272,

recounts scenes of cruelty, as does Heinrich Heine, *De la France* (Paris: Calmann-Lévy, 1884), pp. 138–140. Heine claims to have witnessed the murder of one of the two men killed on the rue de Vaugirard. Old women kicked the dying man with wooden shoes. The body was stripped naked and dragged through the streets to shouts of "This is cholera morbus!" This is the last recorded instance of a clearly ritualized murder. The year 1832 marks a turning point in the treatment of "guilty bodies." Heine referred to those who committed these horrible acts as "savage animals" and "enraged mobs" (p. 139). "No aspect of the populace is more dreadful than the wrath of a mob thirsty for blood and ready to slit the throats of unarmed victims. At such times the streets are awash with a black sea of humanity, out of which workers in their smocks bubble up like crashing white waves."

76. On these violent—but not bloody—episodes, particularly the sack of Dürmenach, see Dominique Lerch, "Imagerie populaire et antisémitisme: Le Haut-Rhin en 1848," *Gazette des beaux-arts* (February 1988): 81–88. In 1832 physical violence accompanied the pillage of Jewish property in the same region.

77. Vigier, *La vie quotidienne,* p. 331.

78. Dusolier, *Ce que j'ai vu,* p. 17.

79. Louis Bernard, known as Télismart de Casseneuil, *Premier recueil de chansons nouvelles* (Bergerac: de Rooy, 1876); Galet, *Meurtre à Hautefaye,* p. 97, proposes a translation of this lament.

80. Ponsac, *Le crime d'Hautefaye,* foreword.

81. Ploux, "Les bagarres," p. 59.

82. Ponsac, *Le crime d'Hautefaye,* p. 4.

83. Letter quoted in Marbeck, *Cent documents,* pp. 77–78.

84. Simonet, *La tragédie du 16 août,* p. 14.

85. Recall the words of François Mazière in Chapter 3: "We killed him. I'm not sorry. We'll kill many more."

86. Letter in Marbeck, *Cent documents,* p. 113.

87. *Echo de la Dordogne,* 28 September 1870.

88. Ponsac, *Le crime d'Hautefaye,* p. 10, on the session of December 15. This account, based on the then-dominant conception of woman, should be treated with caution.

89. Galet, *Meurtre à Hautefaye,* p. 64.

90. Palus, dossier cited, *Arch. Dép. Dordogne* J 1431.

91. Dusolier, *Ce que j'ai vu,* p. 18.

92. Ponsac, *Le crime d'Hautefaye,* pp. 4 and 16.

93. Throughout the trial, the accused pointed out that many of the witnesses ought to have been tried along with them.

94. All quotes from the accused during the trial are taken from Charles Ponsac's published account.
95. *Arch. Nat.* BB24 2037.
96. Simonet, *La tragédie du 16 août,* passim.
97. Lacoste, *Les républicains en Dordogne.*
98. Huard, *Le mouvement républicain,* pp. 397–398.
99. Dusolier, *Ce que j'ai vu,* p. 17.
100. Ibid.
101. Jean Dubois, *Le vocabulaire politique et social en France de 1869 à 1872* (Paris: Larousse, 1962), pp. 59 and 85–87.
102. Quoted in Faury, *Cléricalisme et anticléricalisme,* p. 91.
103. Letter in Marbeck, *Cent documents,* pp. 96ff., which is also the source for the subsequent quotes.
104. Quoted in Marbeck, *Hautefaye, l'année terrible,* p. 315.
105. *Arch. Dép. Dordogne* 1 M 41, dossier on this case.
106. *Arch. Dép. Dordogne* 1 M 41.
107. This aspect of the event is emphasized by Dusolier, *Ce que j'ai vu,* p. 71. In 1874 he contended that this was a "sacred date" (p. 35). Conservatives "will not prevent future generations from appropriately celebrating the anniversary of September 4 as a civic holiday commemorating both the reconquering of liberty and the recovery of honor." It would be interesting to have a more accurate picture of the decline of republican enthusiasm for this "sacred date," this "unprecedented event in the history of nations."
108. Ponsac, *Le crime d'Hautefaye,* foreword.
109. Dusolier, *Ce que j'ai vu,* pp. 18 and 36.
110. A significant statement by General Jaurès, a republican candidate, is quoted in Armengaud, *Les populations de l'Est-aquitaine,* pp. 480–483.
111. Ponsac, *Le crime d'Hautefaye,* foreword.
112. See the closing argument by attorney Millet-Lacombe in Palus, dossier cited, *Arch. Dép. Dordogne* J 1431.
113. Dispatch quoted in Marbeck, *Cent documents,* p. 90.
114. Pointed out by the *procureur général* of the Court of Bordeaux, *Arch. Nat.* BB30 359.
115. *Arch. Nat.* BB24 2037.
116. The three quoted dispatches are from *Arch. Nat.* BB24 2037.
117. *Procureur général,* report of 19 August, *Archives du Service Historique de l'Armée de Terre* (Vincennes) La 8.
118. Reported by Galet, *Meurtre à Hautefaye,* p. 57.
119. Ponsac, *Le crime d'Hautefaye,* p. 5.
120. Bear in mind that this was a jury of the people, although I have not

been able to determine its precise composition. It would be interesting to compare it to the juries of notables that judged those accused of seditious activity under the censitary monarchy. Elisabeth Claverie and Yves Pourcher have shown that nineteenth-century juries, though theoretically representative of the general interest, actually applied standards that reflected local conflicts. See Elisabeth Claverie, "De la difficulté de faire un citoyen: Les 'acquittements scandaleux' du jury dans la France provinciale du début du XIXe siècle," *Etudes rurales* 95–96 (January–June 1984): 143–167; and Yves Pourcher, "Des assises de grâce? Le jury de la Cour d'Assises de la Lozère au XIXe siècle," ibid., pp. 167–181.

121. Bionnier, *Les jacqueries de 1847 en Bas Berry*, p. 104.

122. Galet, *Meurtre à Hautefaye*, pp. 66 and 67.

123. At the rate of once a year, approximately (*Arch. Nat.* F7 3981).

124. Story reconstructed with the aid of Ponsac, *Le crime d'Hautefaye*, and documents in the dossier assembled by Palus, *Arch. Dép. Dordogne* J 1431, together with articles in *Le Nontronnais* and *L'Echo de la Dordogne*, 8 February 1871.

125. According to attorney Biard de Fayemarteau, Hautefaye, interviewed by Gabriel Palus, 16 August 1935.

126. For further information on these final moments, see Palus, *Arch. Dép. Dordogne* J 1431.

127. Well described and analyzed by Arlette Farge, *La vie fragile*, pp. 223–228.

128. Quoted in Marbeck, *Hautefaye, l'année terrible*, p. 318. Unfortunately the author of this document gives no references.

129. Letter in Marbeck, *Cent documents*, pp. 96ff.

130. Ponsac, *Le crime d'Hautefaye*, p. 16.

131. *Arch. Diocésaines* C 55 bis, quoted in Gibson, "Les notables," vol. 1, p. 259.

132. Letter in Marbeck, *Cent documents*, p. 113.

133. Galet, *Meurtre à Hautefaye*, p. 91.

134. In reference to the Saint Bartholomew's Massacre, the Camisards, and the war in Vendée. Joutard is working on the role of memory of conflict in the history of France.

135. For example, the "red virgin" of Var, the inspiration for the character Miette in Zola's *La fortune des Rougon*. See Agulhon, *La République au village*, pp. 455ff. In Hautefaye the relevant female figure was not a political militant but a symbol of the peasantry oppressed by dread of the guillotine and mass execution.

136. *Arch. Nat.* C 3540.

137. Audoin-Rouzeau, *1870*, pp. 303–308.

138. On the battle among various figures of the Republic, see Odile Rudelle, *La République* absolue (Paris: Publications de la Sorbonne, 1982). On the political history of Dordogne in this period, see also the works of Bernard Lachaise.

139. The only way to make real progress in the political history of this period is to begin a thorough investigation into the history of social myths (*l'imaginaire*). Historians must get out of the habit of ascribing to social and regional groups representational systems elaborated by others. Political history has focused too exclusively on ideologies emanating from major urban centers and has paid too little attention to representational and value systems developed in outlying areas and to local reinterpretations of imported ideas. Jean-François Soulet, in his book *Les Pyrénées au XIXe siècle* (Toulouse: Eché, 1987), has been a pioneer in developing a new approach to the subject.

Conclusion

1. Excluding, of course, the period 31 May 1850 to 2 December 1851.

Index